I0224813

NIRVANA

UNCENSORED

ON THE RECORD

BY CAROL CLERK

WITH ADDITIONAL MATERIAL BY
MATTHEW FURNISS AND PETE SOREL-CAMERON

CODA
BOOKS LTD

C⊕DA
BOOKS LTD

www.codabooks.com

This edition is published in Great Britain in 2012 by

Coda Books Ltd., Office Suite 2, Shrieves Walk, 39 Sheep Street, Stratford-upon-Avon, Warwickshire CV37 6GJ

www.codabooks.com

Copyright © 2012 by Coda Books Ltd.

All rights reserved. No part of this publication may be reproduced or transmitted in any form or by any means, electronic or mechanical, including photocopy, recording, or any information storage and retrieval system, without permission in writing from the publisher.

Photographs courtesy of Pictorial Press, Rex Features and PA Photos.

A CIP catalogue record for this book is available from the British Library.

ISBN: 978-1-78158-247-3

MUSIC REVIEWS LTD

CONTENTS

INTRODUCTION

Seattle, Washington State, USA. The "Emerald City", so-called because of its verdant but now declining urban forests; the home of the Space Needle and of coffee culture Starbucks-style; and the rainy birthplace of the nineties' grunge phenomenon, spearheaded by Nirvana - one of the most important rock bands of that or any decade.

Alternative rock may have been around before Nirvana came onto the scene, and bands such as R.E.M., Hüsker Dü, the Pixies, Sonic Youth, Dinosaur Jr. and Butthole Surfers may have pioneered its myriad subgenres and created the blueprint, but it was undoubtedly Kurt Cobain's Nirvana that unintentionally popularised punk, post-punk, and indie rock, bringing it into the American and worldwide mainstream like no other band had done before.

Sitting between Faith Hill and ZZ Top as one of the biggest-selling recording artists in American history, by 1999 Nirvana's breakthrough 1991 album Nevermind had became only the fourth alternative rock album ever to climb to the 10 million sales mark, placing it alongside three other great landmark albums- U2's The Joshua Tree, Pearl Jam's Ten and Green Day's Dookie. In spite of their recording career coming to an impromptu end in 1994, the sales show little sign of slowing down, and the band are as influential and important today as when Nevermind blew everyone's mind back in 1991.

Despite the laboured Seattle connection, the story of Nirvana really belongs to two of Washington State's smaller cities. There's Aberdeen, the place where Kurt Cobain endured a childhood fraught with physical and psychological difficulties that would both blight and drive his musical career; and there's Olympia, where Cobain, a troubled, contradictory adult,

4

launched Nirvana - and unleashed the primal scream that would strike a chord with disaffected teenagers across the world. Arising directly from a tormented soul and a ravaged body, it was a howl of pain and anger, confusion and isolation.

Just as Cobain existed as an outsider in society, so Nirvana considered themselves, and were treated as, outsiders in the bustling Seattle music scene. Their influences and the shape of their music came from a very different environment.

CHAPTER 1

On February 20, 1967, Wendy Cobain gave birth to a blonde-haired, blue-eyed baby boy in Hoquiam, near Aberdeen, Washington. Twenty years later that little boy would become the face of a whole generation. They named him Kurt.

He spent his first months at the family home in nearby Hoquiam with his mother, and his father Donald, a garage mechanic. Within six months they moved to Aberdeen, a city which had enjoyed a thriving economy based on fisheries, shipbuilding and timber - in the 1920s, it was grandly titled the "Lumber Capital of the World", but was now in something of a slump.

The city of Aberdeen is the economic centre of Grays Harbor County and the home port of the tall ship Lady Washington, which featured in the Pirates of the Caribbean movies. Still, for a town of its size Aberdeen is most well-known for its famous people. Painters, Nobel Award-winning physicists, artists, American football players, and novelists rub shoulders with the day-to-dayers in this township founded by early settler Samuel Ben in 1884.

Aberdeen also produced seminal grunge and punk rock bands the Melvins and, of course, Nirvana. The sign that greets people entering this municipality of no more than 20,000 people is inscribed with a tribute to Kurt Cobain: 'Come As You Are', the name of a track on Nevermind. Whether Cobain would have approved of this is neither here nor there; Aberdeen clearly respects its rock heritage.

By the age of three, the young Kurt was showing an affinity for painting and music. A sister, Kimberly, was born in 1970, and all seemed well until Kurt reached the age of seven when he was diagnosed as suffering from hyperactivity.

But something infinitely more disturbing was about to happen to Kurt. His parents' separation and subsequent divorce when he was eight years of age dramatically changed his world-view. He burned with resentment and shame. He wanted his family, not the fractured life that was now to be his lot. At first he lived with his mother. He then moved to his father's new home in Montesano, WA, and in the ensuing years he was tossed around from one set of relatives to another, one school to the next, in a human game of pass the parcel.

In a 1993 interview with Jon Savage for Guitar World, he remembered: "I was very isolated. I had a really good childhood, until the divorce. Then, all of a sudden, my whole world changed. I became anti-social."

The enforced loss of joy, innocence and belonging in his young life haunted Cobain until the day he died. In his suicide note, he wrote: "I have it good, very good, and I'm grateful, but since the age of seven, I've become hateful towards all humans in general. Only because it seems so easy for people to get along that have empathy."

Singled out for his promise, his sensitivity and keen intelligence, Kurt, by his own estimation, was a manic depressive at the age of nine. At ten, he claimed, his life was rubbish and everyone around him was an "asshole".

Those 'assholes' would come to include Wendy's next husband, with whom Cobain had a tempestuous relationship. His father's remarriage was equally destabilising, introducing into his life a stepmother and two step-siblings who only added to his festering insecurities. Reportedly suffering from serious depression before he'd even begun puberty, Cobain would later give voice to his alienation through the words and music of Nirvana.

Kurt developed a series of medical ailments. In his early his teens he was diagnosed with a minor case of scoliosis, a condition which resulted in his spine becoming unnaturally curved. Later, he would suffer from crippling pains in the gut which persisted throughout his life. In his suicide note, he referred to "the pit of my burning nauseous stomach" - whatever his reasons for getting into heroin, it seems that it at least temporarily numbed the agony. He wasn't above using his pain. "Most of the time I sing right from my stomach," he told Jon Savage, "right from where my stomach pain is." Some have suggested that it came from an unhealthy diet. The internal irritation was red and real, but Cobain believed it was a psychosomatic illness triggered by anger and screaming. He told Savage about the scoliosis, explaining that the weight of his guitar had worsened his spinal curvature. He added, "It gives me a back pain all the time. That really adds to the pain in our music... I'm kinda grateful for it."

The young Cobain began drinking, smoking dope and rebelling against the small-town prejudices of Aberdeen, a place full of real-life Beavises and Butt-Heads. By 15, he was becoming deliberately provocative, later telling Advocate magazine "I used to pretend I was gay just to fuck with people.

I've had the reputation of being a homosexual ever since I was 14. It was really cool, because I found a couple of gay friends in Aberdeen - which is almost impossible. How I could ever come across a gay person in Aberdeen is amazing! But I had some really good friends that way. I got beat up a lot, of course, because of my association with them."

"People just thought I was weird at first, just some fucked-up kid. But once I got the gay tag, it gave me the freedom to be able to be a freak and let people know that they should just stay away from me. Instead of having to explain to someone that they should just stay the fuck away from me - I'm gay, so I can't even be touched. It made for quite a few scary experiences in alleys walking home from school, though."

In Nirvana, he would echo that behaviour, playing with gender-blurring imagery and championing gay and women's causes. Instinctively, as a teen, he drifted towards gays and other individuals who, like himself, were marginalised by their peers. Musicians were always interesting to him. They represented non-conformity, spontaneity, excitement and rebellion - all the things that were frowned upon in his home town.

His feelings about Aberdeen undoubtedly shaped his future. "Aberdeen was depressing," he laughed in an interview from the early '90s, "and there were a lot of negative things about it, but it was really fun to fuck with people all the time. I loved to go to parties, jock-keggers, and just run around drunk and obnoxious, smoking cigars and spitting on the backs of these big redneck jocks and them not realising it. By the end of the evening, usually I'd end up offending a girl, and she'd get her boyfriend to come beat me up."

Music was his constant comfort and encouragement. As an infant, listening to The Beatles in his parents' home, he latched on to the irresistibility of pop melody. At 12, happening upon articles about the Sex Pistols, he was instantly attracted to their spiky look and snotty attitude. At around the same time, he went to his first live gig - by Sammy Hagar - where he experienced at first hand the enormous sound of heavy metal thunder. He saw British metal outfit Judas Priest, too. He bought records by Iron Maiden. Pop, punk and crunching rock were the raw materials with which Cobain would build the foundations of Nirvana, adding the unique and feverish twists that would turn them into a band like no other.

He'd started playing instruments early on. He enjoyed banging on the drum given to him by his Aunt Mari - Wendy's sister - when he was seven, so much so that he started taking drum lessons. Aunt Mari's husband, Chuck, presented him with a Lindell guitar for his 14th birthday, and Kurt received tuition from a family friend. Like many a would-be guitar ace before him, he cut his teeth on Led Zeppelin's hippie fantasy 'Stairway To Heaven' as well as other varied morsels by The Kingsmen, AC/DC, The Cars and Queen.

The single most important musical event also happened in that same year: Kurt Cobain met the Melvins.

CHAPTER 2

The Melvins were exponents of the contemporary American spin on punk rock. A three-piece, they played hardcore, loudly and at heart-stopping speed, and they were the biggest noise in Aberdeen. One day at a supermarket in Montesano, Kurt bumped into their singer, Buzz Osborne, who handed him a flyer advertising a free gig the next night in the store's car park. Kurt turned out for the concert, and in the space of that couple of hours, everything changed.

In an interview with Spin magazine, he remembered: "Until I met the Melvins, my life was really boring. All of a sudden, I found a totally different world. I started getting into music and finally seeing shows and doing things I always wanted to do..."

Cobain had never dreamed that music could sound so fast and furious and challenging to not only society but to mainstream rock too. With Buzz's encouragement, he avidly explored albums by hardcore heroes such as the Dead Kennedys, Minutemen, Flipper and Black Flag, the Californian outfit led by Henry Rollins. Black Flag were probably the most influential band in the movement. Later, they would achieve an even greater intensity by slowing down the speed of their songs. The Melvins would follow suit - but never a band to do things by halves, they slowed things down to such a thick, monstrous, murky basic that in 1987, it's said, they invented grunge, or at least its bedrock.

Back then in 1982, Kurt became friends with Buzz and the other Melvins: drummer Dale Crover and bassist Matt Lukin, whose gargantuan appetite for alcohol was matched by a capacity for wreaking havoc wherever he might find a party. He would later join Mudhoney. Cobain was now running with a circle of like-minded people; his schoolteachers would be seeing a lot less of him. He continued to excel in art class, but his twin interests, music and pot, were paramount.

A notorious incident occurred in 1984 at a time when Kurt was once again living at Wendy's home, witnessing the sometimes explosive arguments that erupted between his mother and stepfather. On this occasion, Wendy gathered up her husband's guns and hurled them into the River Wishkah so she couldn't shoot him - Kurt had the guns pulled back out of the water, and he sold or pawned them. With the proceeds, he bought his first amp.

Kurt became homeless later that year when Wendy threw him out of the house. Often, he stayed with friends, Dale Crover for one, and sometimes he slept in public buildings. In May 1985, he walked out of Aberdeen High a month before term's end, despite having won a couple of scholarships to go to art school. "I knew I didn't want to do art," he told Hits magazine in 1991. "I wanted to do music..."

On June 1, he moved into a flat in Aberdeen with a friend. By now, Kurt was writing his own songs. It was during this period too, that he started playing music with Chris Novoselic.

Krist Anthony Novoselic was born on May 16, 1965, in Compton, California. His parents - Marija and Krist, a truck driver – were Croatian immigrants who had met in America a few years before. At first they lived in Gardena, where another son and a daughter were born, before moving to Aberdeen, Washington, when Krist was 14. He adapted his name to Chris, in an effort to fit in with his classmates at Aberdeen High, only changing it back in the later part of Nirvana's career (in this book, he'll be called Krist), but he still found life difficult, having moved from a much more tolerant and relaxed part of America to a place renowned for its preponderance of what he later described as "redneck losers". Krist's towering height – he's six feet seven inches tall -singled him out for special

attention, and despite his clowning antics, he was frequently a target of abuse. His time at the school overlapped with Kurt Cobain's for a while, although since Novoselic was two years older, they spent no time together. Kurt, however, told Melody Maker's Everett True that he remembered Krist from schooldays as a "really clever, funny, loud-mouth person [that] everyone laughed at, even though he was smarter than them".

Like Kurt, Krist later talked about being surrounded by "assholes". His natural high spirits could not rise above the misery of his daily experiences. He sank into a depression, and in June 1980 was sent to live with relations for a year in Yugoslavia, where he first heard the Sex Pistols and the Ramones. Returning to Aberdeen, he took to alcohol and dope with a vengeance, and at 17, saw his first gig, by German metal band The Scorpions, in Seattle. He met his future wife Shelli during his final year in high school, from where he graduated in 1983. That year was a troubled one for Krist, as it also saw his parents divorce and a lengthy operation designed to correct his severe dental overbite.

The next year, he entered into Kurt's orbit when he made friends with the Melvins' Buzz Osborne. For a while, he would become their driver, a duty also undertaken at different times by Cobain - who unsuccessfully auditioned to join the band. But both Kurt and Krist would become involved in some of the Melvins' many satellite projects.

Novoselic was struck by Cobain's cynicism, his creativity and his aptitude for composing melodies that were compelling and different.

Krist has written in his memoir - Of Grunge And Government: Let's Fix This Broken Democracy - that Cobain, when they first met, had his own flat - "a den of art/insanity" - and a job. In fact, Kurt had two part-time jobs around this time. In an unlikely return to school, he became a janitor at Aberdeen High.

He also worked shifts as a children's swimming instructor at the YMCA.

Maybe it was all the acid he was taking. Maybe it was just his usual disinclination to apply himself to anything other than music and drugs. Whatever it was, Kurt was out of work and out of the shared flat by the autumn of 1985 - and the coming winter was the one in which he famously slept outdoors below the bridge that straddled the River Wishkah, as detailed in the Nevermind track "Something In The Way".

Cobain later said in a Spin interview: "I always wanted to experience the street life because my teenage life in Aberdeen was so boring. But I was never really independent enough to do it. I applied for food stamps, lived under the bridge, and built a fort at the cedar mill."

No one really knows if Kurt - an incorrigible myth-maker - actually did this. What does seem indisputable is that before Christmas, Aberdeen High, the school he had quit so casually, was in some way offering a helping hand again, having already employed him as a caretaker. This time, one of its English teachers, Mr Lamont Shillinger, offered him sofa space in his home. Kurt was especially friendly with two of the six-strong Shillinger brood. He jammed with Eric, who had a guitar, and with Steve, a heavy metal fiend, he went out vandalising and spraying graffiti round the streets of Aberdeen. He told Everett True, later a Nirvana biographer, that he would break into people's homes, not to steal anything but just to smash up whatever they had. This, Cobain reckoned, was not only a symptom of boredom but a continuation of the war he had been waging on society since his parents' divorce. He would later channel his rage and frustration, his lust for revenge, through Nirvana.

The surprising thing is that Kurt and his sleeping bag were tolerated for a full eight months on the Shillingers' couch.

He had already started playing seriously, recording a demo tape back in 1982 at his ever-supportive Aunt Mari's home during the Christmas school holidays. Titled Organised Confusion, it featured Cobain singing, screaming, playing guitar and battering a suitcase by way of percussion. There was a muffled, distorted quality about the sound, a weighty bass and a clattering of wooden spoons, but Kurt was not after precision. He was interested in spontaneity and feeling. Offered the use of a computerised drumming aid, he responded, "I want to keep my music pure"; a concept that would remain vitally important to him as the years passed.

One particularly famous demo was also recorded on Aunt Mari's four-track, this one in December 1985. Kurt had formed an occasional band - Fecal Matter - with Melvins' drummer Dale Crover on bass and Greg Hokanson on drums. Legend has it that Fecal Matter actually played a gig supporting the Melvins, and possibly several other shows, before Greg's departure. Whatever the truth, it was Kurt and Dale who spent two days recording at Mari's place, with Crover on this occasion playing drums.

The resulting tape included two embryonic Nirvana songs: 'Downer' and 'Spank Thru', which both regularly featured in the band's early performances. From these Fecal Matter sessions, 'Spank Thru' was officially released on the 2005 compilation, Sliver - The Best Of The Box.

Mari later described the material to Gillian G Gaar, writing for the record collector's magazine Goldmine: "The guitar riffs were fast and furious, with a powerful hook. The lyrical content was rebellious and angry, mostly slams against society in general. Kurt didn't like the social ladder in school - kids thinking they were cool because they wore the 'right' clothes or were handsome or pretty, or had money."

Cobain and Crover made cassette copies of the recordings

and packaged them with a title of Illiteracy Will Prevail. However, Fecal Matter didn't last much beyond their next line-up, featuring Buzz Osborne on bass and Mike Dillard, the Melvins' first drummer, at the kit.

Kurt, meanwhile, gave a copy of the tape to Chris Novoselic, who was especially impressed by 'Spank Thru': "It got me excited, so I go, 'Hey man, let's start a band.'"

They took it all very seriously, but their first attempts amounted to little. There were The Sellouts who, with Kurt on drums, Krist on vocals and Steve Newman on bass, played covers of swampy rock'n'roll songs by Creedence Clearwater Revival. Kurt and Krist took on the same roles in another band, a sometime Melvins project called the Stiff Woodies.

Cobain explained: "we had various side bands with Buzz Osborne, then the Melvins, other members of the Melvins, and friends of ours. We got together and played in a few bands like the Stiff Woodies. We'd play at local jock-kegs. We'd put Knox gel in our hair like [English new wavers] GBH and play live music at these parties. It was great. We freaked everybody out. But everyone was so drunk that they didn't care about our appearance. They just wanted live music," he said, adding, "If we played together in the house for a couple of hours and two people stopped by, we considered that a gig."

Eventually deciding on Skid Row as the band's name, Cobain and Novoselic, along with Aaran Burkhart on drums, played their first official gig at a local party in the woods of Aberdeen. Kurt recalled, "It was pretty amazing. That was a fun night. I think it was Halloween night. We were really drunk, and we had some fake Halloween blood and we smeared it all over ourselves and played our seven songs off the tape. And we alienated the entire crowd. The entire party moved into the kitchen and left the band, just left us there in the front room playing our songs."

This musical partnership was cut short when Krist and Shelli set off for Phoenix, Arizona, to try and build a more prosperous life for themselves. However, the venture was ill-fated and they returned to Washington six months later, prompting the continuation of the friendship and the creative relationship that would eventually become Nirvana.

During Krist's absence, two things had happened in Seattle. Sub Pop Records was launched in July 1986 by Bruce Pavitt with the release of a compilation album. Pavitt had formerly run a fanzine called Subterranean Pop, and through it released some cassettes of local independent music. His second Sub Pop release was by the now-legendary band Green River, which included future members of Mudhoney and Pearl Jam. Shortly afterwards, Pavitt went into partnership with Jonathan Poneman, a club promoter and radio presenter who gave airtime to demos by unsigned bands. At the time, Poneman was championing a local group called Soundgarden.

That July also saw the opening of the Reciprocal Recording studio, which would later become home to Nirvana.

In August, Kurt left the Shillingers' house at their request, reportedly after a fight, and bummed around on friends' sofas before his mother lent him the deposit and the first month's rent for another flat in Aberdeen, nicknamed 'The Shack'. One can only imagine the chaos created there by Kurt - who kept a bath full of turtles in the living room - and his flatmate Matt Lukin, the wild man of the Melvins, especially when the apartment became a regular stop on the punk-rock party circuit. Kurt - often seen as quiet and introspective - was equally capable of wild behaviour. He continued spray-painting Aberdeen, and was arrested for emblazoning random cars with messages reading "God Is Gay" and "Homo Sex Rules". He later recalled, "That was a lot of fun. The funniest thing about that was not actually the act but the next morning. I'd get up early in the morning to walk through the neighbourhood that I'd terrorised to see the aftermath. That was the worst thing I could have spray-painted on their cars. Nothing else would have been more effective." Still, he tried to shoulder his financial responsibilities by taking a job at a local hotel.

It was inevitable that, eventually, Kurt would start playing live. The Melvins were the sort of people who liked to goof around. When they had gigs, they would often put together fun support bands involving their own friends. One such group was Brown Cow. A one-off, they consisted of Melvins Buzz Osborne and Dale Crover, on guitar and drums respectively, and Kurt Cobain singing. It was the winter of 1986 and the venue, in Olympia, was a warehouse space called GESCCO, funded by the city's Evergreen State College.

It would be nice to say that Kurt's performance made a lasting impression on everyone who saw it, but it didn't. GESSCO's Slim Moon, who founded Olympia's kill rock stars label and played in bands himself, recalls seeing Cobain onstage in his everyday grey trench coat and the distinct lack of an audience, but he remembers nothing at all about the music.

When Kurt played his next landmark gig - at a house party in Raymond, Washington, in March 1987 - the bass player was Krist Novoselic. Nirvana had been born in all but name.

Cobain and Novoselic had much in common. Growing up in California, Krist and his brother Robert had indulged in their share of petty vandalism. Novoselic drank to excess, and he smoked dope. He developed a reputation for playing the fool at every party, falling over, taking his clothes off, dancing on tabletops and setting off fire extinguishers. Like Kurt - who'd by now, as a statement, grown his hair - Krist had no time for uniforms of any kind, particularly punk uniforms: to look like every other punk he felt rather missed the point. Furthermore, Cobain and Novoselic had grown frustrated by the rigidity of hardcore (now a dominating musical force, along with heavy metal, in big cities such as Seattle), while still prizing punk's founding principles of volume, protest, self-expression, independence and mayhem. Novoselic unapologetically upheld his allegiance to classic rock bands such as Led Zeppelin, Black Sabbath and Aerosmith.

For the gig at the Raymond party, the drummer was Aaron Burckhard. A member of the Melvins' circle, Aaron was a hearty drinker who would remain with the trio until the autumn. The set included 'Downer" and 'Spank Thru' as well as 'Aero Zeppelin', If You Must', 'Mexican Seafood', 'How Many More Times', 'Pen Cap Chew', 'Hairspray Queen' and 'Heartbreaker'. The hearty if ham-fisted version of Led Zeppelin's 'Heartbreaker', with Kurt in full Banshee mode, was subsequently released on 2004's rarities box set, With The Lights Out. Different versions of 'Aero Zeppelin', 'Mexican Seafood' and 'Hairspray Queen' would later emerge on Incesticide, a compilation of rarities issued in 1992.

Accounts of the gig tell of Krist, characteristically intoxicated, diving out of a window covered in fake blood without missing a note, while Kurt scaled the furniture, sloshing beer around the room as he went.

Cobain later talked to Options about the gig, recalling: "We were really drunk so we started making spectacles of ourselves. Playing off the bad vibes we were giving to the rednecks, you know - jumping off tables and pretending we were rock stars... Then we started playing 'Sex Bomb' [a Flipper cover] for about an hour and our girlfriends were hanging on us and grabbing our legs and doing a mock lesbian scene, and that really started freaking out the rednecks."

The band may have played some other house parties. Certainly they appeared at the Community World Theatre in Tacoma in March under the name of Skid Row.

Slim Moon, founder of the 'kill rock stars' label, described Skid Row to Everett True: "They played really heavy. Kurt was totally glammed out - he was in platform shoes, like a parody of a glam costume... Their songs were basically riffs. They'd play a riff for a long time and Kurt would scream into the microphone, then he'd drop the guitar and play with the digital delay and make crazy noises instead of a guitar solo, and then he'd pick the guitar back up and play the riff some more and scream some more. Right away, he was a showman."

Soon afterwards, the band played the closing gig at GESCCO, which because of an insurance problem had had its funding withdrawn by the College. On that occasion, Novoselic was so drunk that the group were almost banned from performing.

Skid Row's first live radio performance, for KAOS-FM, Evergreen State College's well-regarded station, took place on April 17. They played 'Love Buzz', 'Floyd The Barber', 'Downer', 'Mexican Seafood', 'White Lace And Strange', 'Spank Thru'', 'Anorexorcist', 'Hairspray Queen', 'Pen Cap Chew' and 'Help Me, I'm Hungry'. All but the final track were transmitted. Three recordings from the session were later released on With The Lights Out: 'White Lace And Strange', 'Anorexorcist' and 'Help Me, I'm Hungry'.

Skid Row's songs were typical of early Cobain material, with the singer gasping and roaring while the group crash, bang and wallop along ferociously without drawing breath. It was all very commendable in a punk kind of way but certainly not the incendiary rock of their later legend.

The band would go on to record 'Floyd The Barber' for Bleach, as well as 'Love Buzz', which would be their first single. This was a unique take on a song by Dutch pop band Shocking Blue, best known for their 1970 hit single, 'Venus'. 'Love Buzz' was included on some formats of Bleach.

The radio producer, John Goodmanson, had seen Skid

Row at the final GESCCO night, where he pronounced them "awesome", adding: "They were like an Olympia band. They were obviously the best of the Northwest rock bands - they transcended the whole Seattle Seventies cock-rock macho thing. So we invited them in."

With these initial gigs, Kurt Cobain was not only making a name for himself as a musician, he was dispelling a few myths about himself as an Aberdonian. The people of Aberdeen were looked upon as a breed apart by their "superiors" in centres such as Seattle and Olympia. Aberdeen was a run-down, working-class city with above-average unemployment, so poor that even beggars avoided it. According to Krist Novoselic, Buzz Osborne was "the punk rock guru of Aberdeen".

The Melvins always travelled with an entourage of people from their hometown, described by Slim Moon as "inbred Aberdeen retards" and "scary, loser, freako weirdos". Novoselic escaped such damning judgement; he was larger-than-life, well-known and respected as a bona fide part of the band's inner circle. He'd done a lot of driving for the Melvins, and he'd been the singer in one of their fun projects, The Meltors - who parodied The Mentors, themselves a comic hardcore band.

Outside of Aberdeen, Kurt was initially dismissed as just another of the Melvins' hangers-on. In the end, with the group that would become Nirvana, his actions spoke louder than words.

Meanwhile, back at The Shack, things were not going too well. Cobain was getting fed up with his flatmate Matt Lukin who, around this time in the spring of 1987, left the Melvins. Lukin moved out, and Kurt found a replacement in Dylan Carlson, a friend of Slim Moon's and a young man memorably described by Everett True as "a self-taught genius with wild, unkempt hair, a messy beard and strong views on life".

Come the autumn, Kurt and Krist were searching for a new

drummer. Some reports say that Aaron Burckhard wanted to leave because he found their frequent rehearsals too much of a responsibility. Other sources insist that his drinking had become too wild even for Cobain and Novoselic. No slouches themselves when it came to alcohol, they demanded that the music, and not the party, had to come first. They ran a classified ad in Seattle's leading music publication, the Rocket. It read: "SERIOUS DRUMMER WANTED. Underground attitude, Black Flag, Melvins, Zeppelin, Scratch Acid, Ethel Merman. Versatile as heck."

It gave Cobain's home phone number and showed his name spelt as Kurdt, an affectation that he kept up for quite some time. It also confirmed that he was now living in Olympia; Kurt had started a relationship with his first proper girlfriend, Tracy Marander and when she moved to Olympia, Kurt went with her. They spent little time together, though. Tracy worked nights in a cafeteria at the nearby Boeing plant (along with Shelli, who by now was living in Tacoma with Novoselic) and she slept through the day. Kurt occasionally worked as a cleaner, although he spent most of his time rehearsing, writing songs, listening to music, watching TV or moping around. Tracy left lists of chores for him to do, although it's unlikely he got around to carrying out many of them. He wasn't lonely unless he wanted to be. His neighbours included Slim Moon and Dylan Carlson, who would later play together in the highly regarded band Earth, pioneers of a repetitive, minimalistic, hardcore-influenced music that would become known as Drone.

Olympia was much more of a music city than Aberdeen, with gigs and festivals going on in dozens of clubs and bars and parties. Sub Pop founder Bruce Pavitt had studied in Olympia, where he'd also started his fanzine, Subterranean Pop, and worked in a record shop. There were also two influential independent record labels; K Records run by Calvin Johnson, who also fronted the revered and unconventional Olympia band Beat Happening; and "kill rock stars", Slim Moon's baby, deliberately spelt without capital letters to register punk's vital opposition to star worship and corporate rock.

In comparison to the Seattle scene, which seemed entirely entrenched in the formal delivery of heavy rock and hardcore and was also considered unduly macho, the Olympia bands were experimental and interested in equality: women were welcomed into the world of live performance, and respected. There was a pop sensibility, too, about the city, with The Vaselines and The Pastels enjoying popularity.

Slim Moon summed up the differences between the two cities succinctly: "Seattleites always wanted it big and loud and in leather pants. Olympia always wanted it minimal and naked."

In Olympia, the emphasis was very much on impulsiveness and self-expression as opposed to musical expertise. Many of the groups thought a bass player unnecessary - a revolutionary idea back then.

Bruce Pavitt told Everett True: "There was a real purity about the vision coming out of the Olympia scene, a high level of integrity, while the Seattle scene was more about business. Kurt was schooled in Olympia. Kurt made money in Seattle. That's how I would define it."

Cobain and Novoselic didn't get the response they'd hoped for from their Rocket ad. In December 1987, they called on their old Melvins friend Dale Crover to step in on drums during a few weeks of intensive rehearsing. One track from those rehearsals - 'Mrs Butterworth', a furiously paced twisted anthem of alienation, anger and disgust - was later released on With The Lights Out.

On January 23, 1988, the band went into Reciprocal Recording in Seattle to make a professional demo tape. It set them back $152.44. Their producer Jack Endino knew what they were aiming for since he was in a pioneering grunge band called Skin Yard and had recently produced an EP for Soundgarden. Within the space of a few days that January, he worked with Mother Love Bone (featuring Stone Gossard and Jeff Ament, previously of Green River and later of Pearl Jam), Mudhoney and the future Nirvana.

They recorded and mixed 10 tracks in a single afternoon. Endino later recalled: "He just said, 'Hi, my name is Kurt. I'm from Aberdeen and I'm friends with the Melvins. We want to come in and record some songs really fast; we've got Dale Crover from the Melvins helping us out on drums.' And I thought, well, it's not going to be some shitty band if Dale's playing with them - 'Yeah, come on up' ... It was the best thing I'd heard in a while at the studio."

Endino also told Everett True: "That demo was Seventies riff rock with a slightly weird post-punk angularity. Dale was fundamentally a heavy metal drummer, and Kurt wrote songs around interesting guitar riffs. The thing that separated it from anything else was the singing. His voice had a lot of character and he had a weird ear for melody, he wouldn't be following the guitar riffs like typical idiot riff rock. Right off, I thought, Kurt's got a cool scream."

Because of their collected punk leanings, and the desire to reject the hair metal favoured by MTV at the time, the raw sound of these early recordings was ideally suited to the band. It was a type of rock music that didn't need layers of overdubs and retakes to make it perfect; it was instant and real, with all the passion of a live act. Krist and Kurt were also desperate to have an end product for their labours. At this stage in the band's development, they wanted something they could hold in their hands as their own creation, and the demo was exactly that. The tape would also be the key to the band breaking into the Seattle music scene, and would effectively start them on the road to fame, as it circulated behind the scenes of the local music industry.

The completed songs were: 'If You Must', 'Pen Cap Chew', 'Spank Thru', 'Downer', 'Floyd The Barber', 'Paper Cuts', 'Hairspray Queen', 'Aero Zeppelin', 'Beeswax' and 'Mexican Seafood'.

Almost all of the songs from this session have been released commercially. 'Floyd The Barber' and 'Paper Cuts' were included on Bleach, with 'Downer' appearing on some formats. 'Hairspray Queen' and 'Aero Zeppelin' emerged on Incesticide, 'Beeswax' first appeared on a kill rock stars compilation, 'Mexican Seafood' turned up on C/Z Records' 1989 compilation EP Teriyaki Asthma Vol. 1 and 'If You Must' and 'Pen Cap Chew' were issued on With The Lights Out.

Having completed the recordings, the band dashed off to Tacoma for a gig, once again at the Community World Theatre, billed as Ted, Ed, Fred. It was Crover's last gig with Kurt and Krist: The Melvins were regrouping in San Francisco, without Matt Lukin, and Crover was getting on board.

Although Nirvana is the most renowned and recognised grunge band, they weren't the most influential. Before Nirvana there were a number of acts that paved the way for what would become a global sensation. Perhaps the most important group for the beginnings of the movement was Green River. They are revered for a number of reasons, the first and most obvious of which is that Mark Arm, the band's frontman, is credited with first using the term 'grunge' to sum up a musical style. In describing their sound as 'pure grunge, pure shit', he wasn't simply coining a catchy word for a new genre, he was outlining the mood of the music: self-deprecating and despondent, while at the same time angry and outspoken.

As well as this, after Green River split in 1987, the individual members went on to start their own bands, each of which would become an important component of the rising popularity of Seattle music in the late 80s and early 90s. Mark Arm and guitarist Steve Turner went on to form Mudhoney, with Matt Lukin. Bassist Jeff Ament and guitarists Stone Gossard and Bruce Fairweather formed Mother Love Bone, which, after the death of the band's singer, Andrew Wood, reincarnated as Pearl Jam, a band that would go on to become as universally popular and famous as Nirvana.

This was the start of a movement, and in Seattle in 1988, the music scene was gearing up for an explosion. Bands such as Mudhoney, Mother Love Bone and Soundgarden were making waves, starting to get noticed on a scale unheard of for bands from the region. Mother Love Bone had signed to Polygram and were set to release an EP followed by an album, both of which were eagerly anticipated. Soundgarden had released two EPs on Sub Pop, and then signed to SST Records. Mudhoney, also on Sub Pop, had released a single and the Superfuzz Bigmuff EP, which would have a huge impact on the grunge scene and, more specifically, on Nirvana. Collectively, these groups were beginning to make Seattle something of a musical epicentre, and it was here that the newly named Nirvana would find their first big fan base.

Kurt had sent off mountains of demos to almost every record company in America, but none had replied. It seemed as though The Melvins had the right idea when they left for California - no-one seemed interested in what grunge acts had to say; at least none of the major labels.

Endino, meanwhile, was so impressed by the tapes that Nirvana had cut at his studio that he remixed the recordings and passed copies to a handful of friends, all of whom responded quickly. The most important recipient was Jonathan Poneman: the Sub Pop men were always interested in the bands passing through Reciprocal Recording.

Talking to author Carrie Borzillo, Poneman recalled: "He [Endino] told me, 'There's this kid who came in who looks like a car mechanic. He came in with Dale Crover. He lives in Olympia and his name is Kurt.' And he says, 'To be honest, I don't even really know what to make of this tape. It's awesome, but they just bashed it out and it's really unlike anything I've really heard. The guy's got an amazing voice.'"

In an interview with Everett True, Poneman described his first experience of Nirvana: "I remember listening to the first song, 'If You Must', and going, 'This is kind of cool, nice guitar riff, mumbly Tom Petty-like vocals... and then I came to that crescendo, that 'RAAAA'! It was the first time I heard Kurt's roar. I sat there looking at the tape deck going, 'Oh my God!' I literally popped the tape out of the deck and rushed down to the offices where Bruce [Pavitt] was working: 'You have got to listen to this tape.'"

Pavitt wasn't convinced straight away: he didn't think the songs were up to much.

More enthusiastic was writer Dawn Anderson, who would become the band's first supporter in the local rock press. She'd started up a fanzine, Backlash, writing about the new breed of longhairs such as Skin Yard, Mudhoney, Soundgarden and Mother Love Bone. Now there was Cobain's three-piece and, later, Tad.

Another recipient of the tape was Shirley Carlson, a presenter at Seattle's KCMU radio station, who immediately began giving 'Floyd The Barber' some late-night airplay.

Kurt, meanwhile, was handing copies to his friends, among them Slim Moon. Moon told Carrie Borzillo, "I played it a lot and I thought it was great. I hadn't really realized how good they were... Kurt was a lot better songwriter than I had realised. I didn't really think he had that much ambition then, but I got to know him better and I sort of realised that he really did." Cobain also sent tapes and letters to his favourite Indie labels with little response. However, Jonathan Poneman still had the bit between his teeth. He wanted the band to record for Sub Pop.

Yet again, they needed a drummer, and they took out another classified ad in the Rocket. It specified, "DRUMMER WANTED: Play hard, sometimes light, underground, versatile, fast, medium, slow, versatile, serious, heavy, versatile, dorky, nirvana, hungry."

In the meantime, they tried out a guy from Aberdeen who'd been recommended by Dale Crover before he left. Dave Foster was a jazz drumming student and a heavy metal freak. Two things stood out about him: he had a truck and he had a moustache. One was good, the other wasn't. Even worse than the moustache was his explosively bad temper; it was so bad Slim Moon and Dylan Carlson nicknamed him 'Anger Problem Dave'.

The band's first gig with Anger Problem Dave was at Olympia's Caddyshack. They also played in the library at Evergreen State College, where local musician Nikki McClure immediately imagined their future in terms of massive arenas and flickering lighter flames. "They had 'it'," she told Everett True. "I knew they'd be totally huge."

On March 19, the band played a significant gig at Tacoma Community World Theatre, appearing for the first time as Nirvana. The name was splashed across the top of the flyers in big letters, with an explanation underneath in small writing: "Also known as Skid Row, Ted Ed Fred, Pen Cap Chew, and Bliss."

Nirvana were joined on the bill by Lush - Slim Moon's band at the time- and other special guests in what was probably intended to be some sort of spiritual and charitable extravaganza. Fans were instructed that if they brought along cans of food they would have money knocked off the price of admission, while an announcement elsewhere on the flyer advised: "Hey kids!

Don't buy a gram this weekend. Come and see a revelation in progress. It will be a gosh darn healing Explosion."

By now, fans were used to seeing Kurt in all his sartorial splendour, a riotous, multi-layered mix of female clothing and second-hand chic. This satisfied several purposes, not least the "redneck" wind-up factor. It was also Kurt's way of embracing the feminine, and of sneering at the more contrived preening of traditional rock stars.

Chad Channing was in the audience that night, and he later described the gig to Carrie Borzillo: "The sound was really bad; it was really, really noisy. I liked the way they looked more than the way they sounded... Kurt was wearing these high heels and had these really intense bellbottoms on. But I couldn't really make too much heads or tails on what exactly they were playing. It was a combination of just the sound and the room and everything else; when I heard them the second time, I got a little more of an understanding of what was going on... I got into it when they gave me the tape they did with Dale.I knew things were going to happen for them."

Nirvana's first gig in Seattle in March 1988 was a tiny affair attended, some say, by only three people: Jonathan Poneman, Bruce Pavitt, and the barman - some argue that a few other souls were there. Poneman had arranged a gig at the Central Tavern with a view to releasing a Nirvana record on Sub Pop. He had hoped that the band, live, would convert Pavitt.

"Their songs were bad," said Pavitt, who was largely unconverted, to Everett True. "But Kurt had a good voice. They played one good song, and it was by Shocking Blue. None of their original material was outstanding in the least. I thought we could probably get away with putting the cover out."

Poneman remembers that Kurt threw up. This would become a normal feature of Nirvana gigs, apparently a by-product of the singer's stomach problems.

The drummer on this occasion was Aaron Burckhard. Unbeknown to Dave Foster, Kurt and Chris were once again rehearsing with Aaron, but it was an ill-fated reunion. After a drunken escapade involving Kurt's car, a cop, a police cell and an almighty hangover, Burckhard was once again invited to leave Nirvana.

Dave Foster was back behind the kit for the gig that's usually flagged as the band's first in Seattle. It took place at The Vogue on April 24, with 'Love Buzz' opening a set of 14 songs. There was a modest audience including various musicians. For those people, and for Nirvana themselves, it was not an auspicious event. Kurt later complained that it felt like the band was on trial.

Dawn Anderson turned up to review it for the Rocket and to write about Nirvana for Backlash. It was their first interview and photo session. Dawn wasn't hugely impressed by the performance, although she made allowances for Cobain, who revealed to her that pains in his stomach had made him sick that afternoon. She stated in her review that Kurt "was so nervous that he was shaking in his flannels". Interviewing him, she found him quiet, shy and somewhat bewildered by the attention he was receiving.

Sub Pop's photographer Charles Peterson - the man whose shots of interacting bands and audiences on the record sleeves created a unique identity for the label - was appalled by Nirvana, famously deciding not to take any shots of the performance. And one of the Rocket's editors walked out of the gig, declaring it "dreadful" on the grounds that the songs all sounded the same. Despite this, the initially sceptical Bruce Pavitt was getting to like the idea of releasing 'Love Buzz' as a seven-inch.

CHAPTER 3

The original agreement was for one single, and there could be no debate: it had to be 'Love Buzz'. Cobain later reasoned: "It was a pop song. It was one of the only palatable songs that we had. At the time we were writing stuff like 'Hairspray Queen'. Even though there was a little bit of pop element in some of the songs, we thought we'd get instant attention by that. It was such a catchy song and it was so repetitive that we thought that people would listen to it right away and remember it."

There was no contract. Sub Pop was too indie, too punk, too alternative to go in for anything so corporate. Deals were done on a handshake. There was no formal office structure - no archiving and precious little accounting or filing. Sub Pop ran on idealism, imagination, adrenalin, foresight, trust and goodwill.

Kurt Cobain was worried by this. He felt that Sub Pop was showing no commitment to the band or its music, firstly because they were offering only to release a single, and secondly because they would not consider an original song for the A-side. It was insulting. For Jonathan Poneman, an eager fan, it was a necessary compromise. It allowed him to bring Nirvana to the label without ruffling anybody's feathers, especially Pavitt's, in the hope that the company and the record-buyers would warm to the band eventually.

Cobain was anxious, too, about the lack of business acumen among the people running the label, its dismal finances and his suspicion that the lion's share of any spare cash that Sub Pop might have would be invested in Mudhoney, which at that time was much the bigger band. Pavitt later insisted that everything he possibly could have done for any of his bands he did, and then some.

Nirvana had received no better offers, and they warily entered into the pact with Sub Pop. Now they had to prove themselves to small crowds and to the cliquey circles of music folk around Sub Pop and Seattle. It was a struggle at first. For every conquest, there would be someone else sticking the knife in: they were too loud, too inept; they were Melvins wannabes.

Candice Peterson, girlfriend of K Records' Calvin Johnson, was a regular at the band's Tacoma gigs. She told Everett True what some of the snobbier Seattle types had been missing about Nirvana: "They were bad and stupid - silly and outrageous and fucked-up all the time. Not like fucked-up people, but they fucked up every song. It was pure stupidity, it was how rock'n'roll should be - stupid and fun."

In the summer of 1988 Nirvana returned to the Central Tavern, where they had memorably played their lower-than-low-key performance for Poneman and Pavitt. On this night they opened for Leaving Trains whose singer, Falling James, would become the first Mr Courtney Love.

Falling James was enthralled by Nirvana, later telling Carrie Borzillo: "I identified with them for many reasons, including the spontaneous excitement of witnessing for the first time a bunch of simpatico longer-haired slacker types who just didn't give a fuck about image or the then-current faux-metal revival, or making it. They reminded me of me. But I felt oddly liberated to see how Nirvana took punk energy and inspiration and ideals, and transmuted them into something different, something chaotic and beautiful. I was jealous and proud of them, and felt like I was a part of it somehow."

Everyone, but everyone, mentioned Kurt's anguished wail.

By now, Nirvana had rid themselves of Dave Foster and his moustache. When out drinking one night in Aberdeen, Foster got into a fight, for which he was arrested and had to spend two weeks in jail. With a lot of rehearsal required prior to the recording session, this posed a huge problem for the band, and so Kurt and Krist decided it was time for another drummer change.

Kurt and Krist settled on Bainbridge Island drummer Chad Channing, who'd talked with the band after watching them perform at Olympia's Evergreen State College. There, they had asked if he fancied playing with them. He did.

Chad was very close to Kurt's age. He was born on New Year's Eve, 1967, in Santa Rosa, California, to Burnyce and Wayne, a TV newscaster and radio presenter. The nature of Wayne's world meant that the family rarely lived in one place for long, their travels taking them everywhere from Alaska to Hawaii. Chad suffered a major blow when a broken leg put paid to his dreams of becoming a soccer player, so he turned from sport to music, learning drums and guitar, and played in a series of bands. One of these, the Melvins-influenced Mind

Circus, featured guitarist Ben Shepherd, who would later join Soundgarden on bass. When Chad was 17, he played in a speed metal band called Stone Crow. By the time he bumped into Nirvana, his parents had split and he was scraping a living as a cook.

On June 11 1988, Nirvana went into Reciprocal Recording with Jack Endino, who was quickly becoming Sub Pop's regular producer. Endino would later receive great credit for his part in Seattle's grunge movement. This was the first of three sessions for Nirvana's début single, the others taking place on June 30 and July 16. They recorded 'Love Buzz' for the A-side, choosing the second take, and as the B-side, 'Big Cheese' - Kurt's song of complaint about Jonathan Poneman's "judgemental" attitude, according to author Michael Azerrad. They also taped 'Mr Moustache', 'Blew', an instrumental rendition of 'Sifting', 'Floyd The Barber', 'Spank Thru' and 'Blandest'. This recording of 'Spank Thru' was released soon afterwards, in December 1988, as part of the three-EP compilation set, Sub Pop 200. 'Blandest' appears on the more recent With The Lights Out.

Nirvana played around Washington throughout the summer, earning around $50 a night. Generally, the shows were not well attended; yet for the band, these were some of their happiest times. On June 29, they appeared with Tad and Mudhoney at a Sub Pop Lame Fest, held in Seattle's Moore Theater. Paul De Barros, reviewing for the Seattle Times, said tartly: "If this is the future of rock'n'roll... I hope I die before I get much older."

Dawn Anderson's Backlash feature about Nirvana was published in August. Despite her misgivings about the gig she'd seen at The Vogue, she stuck her neck out, advising that "with enough practice, Nirvana could become bigger than the Melvins."

This was followed later the same month by a piece in the

Tacoma News Tribune about the rise of Pacific Northwest bands including Screaming Trees, an Ellensburg band who'd been picked up by the ultra-cool label SST; and Soundgarden, who'd moved from Sub Pop to SST and would later go on to make their major breakthrough on A&M Records. The Seattle audiences started growing.

By the autumn of 1988, Nirvana were getting wilder onstage. On October 28, they appeared at Union Station with the Butthole Surfers and Blood Circus, after which the owner stopped hosting gigs. Two nights later, they were on a bill with Lush, celebrating Halloween at Evergreen State College. Lush staged a memorable performance which exploded into a fight onstage, with the drummer punching Slim Moon full in the face. They might have hoped, on that one occasion, that they'd done enough to blow Nirvana off, but they had reckoned without Kurt Cobain, who, drenched in fake blood, smashed his guitar to pieces at the end of the show. Moon has since admitted that he felt hurt by Kurt's apparent refusal to let anyone, even a friend, upstage Nirvana.

Although Cobain is reported to have bashed his guitar around on previous occasions, this is thought to be the first time he actually wrecked it. Equipment-smashing would become a regular feature of Nirvana's set, with Kurt forever having to get his guitars repaired or replaced with cheap models, since the band was certainly not rich at the time, and guitars have never been cheap. Clearly, this was a stupid idea financially but in terms of mood, it summed up the anger and emotion that typified the band's music. Watching a man give such a raw, powerful performance in such a confined space, and then, rather than politely thanking the audience and going back to being a mild-mannered party-goer - putting the anger back in the box - to see him follow through and work his anger out on the objects around him symbolised the potency of Nirvana's music, an image made all the more potent because other rock groups of the time tended to gloss over the frustration felt by American youth.

Sub Pop's Megan Jasper said to Everett True: "Those early shows were crazy and that's why they were so fun. It ruled, the way Kurt would smash up his guitars at every opportunity - we all knew he didn't have any money, but he'd do it anyway."

The label's former general manager Rich Jensen told True: "One of the first Nirvana shows I saw was at The Vogue, either with Pussy Galore or Tad, at a Sub Pop showcase. At the end, they smashed up all of their gear. Apparently, that was something Kurt would prepare for. Ian Dickson [Sub Pop's computer whiz kid] told me his amps were all pre-broken so he could jump into them and smash them, and do it again and again."

'Love Buzz' was released in November and, true to its title, it created an instant wave of interest, not only in Washington but across the Atlantic, in Britain. Melody Maker journalist Everett True made it one of three US Singles Of The Week.

He wrote: "Nirvana are beauty incarnate. A relentless two-chord garage beat which lays down some serious foundations for a sheer monster of a guitar force to howl over. The volume control ain't been built yet which can do justice to this three-piece! WHAT IS GOING DOWN OVER THERE? Somebody pass me a gun. Limited edition of a thousand; love songs for the psychotically disturbed."

In his biography, Nirvana: The True Story, Everett added: "Here were bands that achieved what I had thought hitherto impossible: they made metal sound cool... Up until grunge there had always been a line drawn between popular and underground music; Journey on one side, Dead Kennedys on the other. People got beat up for being punk rock, especially in the US. Sub Pop blurred that line once and for all."

'Love Buzz' was issued as the first in a series of 'Singles

Club' releases. Fans were invited to pay $35 a year, in return for which they would be sent a new Sub Pop single every month. For his part, Kurt Cobain was miffed that Nirvana's debut single was to receive such a limited release.

The effect of 'Love Buzz' in the immediate vicinity was to challenge various perceptions of the band and bring the music to a wider audience. Craig Montgomery, later to become Nirvana's sound engineer, confirmed to Carrie Borzillo that in Seattle, there existed a widely-held opinion of Nirvana as "hicks from the woods". He added: "But the thing that first made the impression was Kurt's voice. It was like, 'Wow, it's this Creedence Clearwater kind of voice from these hick guys from Aberdeen.'"

Jonathan Poneman remarked to Borzillo: "We realised that people were reacting like, 'Yeah, this is really, really great." But I don't think Bruce and I realized that the band was going to be as big as they ended up being."

Kurt and Krist had an incredible sense of urgency in the band's early stages. It was this urgency that compelled them to put the band before anything else in their lives. Kurt regularly drove hundreds of miles so that every member of the group could attend three practice sessions a week, and they would both spend a lot of money to ensure the name Nirvana was promoted to the right people, in the right way. They made endless sacrifices to make the band an integral part of the Northwest music scene, and their early dealings with Sub Pop were just one component of these efforts.

Charles R Cross, editor of the Rocket and a future Nirvana biographer, told Borzillo that in these early days, Nirvana were treated like "poor stepbrothers to Mudhoney" by their peers and by Sub Pop, and that this imbalance started changing with 'Love Buzz'. Cross also said: " 'Love Buzz' was notable mostly for the guitar playing and that's what people forget about early

Nirvana - the main reason people were interested in the band was because of the guitar playing. In the club settings, the vocals were virtually impossible to hear."

Another large attraction – literally - of Nirvana was Krist Novoselic. Many spectators found his drunken buffoonery more visually interesting than anything Kurt was doing onstage, bar the guitar smashing. Dawn Anderson, when she first met the band, had seen Novoselic as more of a spokesman and natural leader than Cobain, while recognising the latter's creative drive.

In December, Nirvana filmed a practice in Krist's mother's home, with Robert Novoselic behind the video camera. They played 'Love Buzz', 'Scoff', 'About A Girl', 'Big Long Now', Led Zeppelin's 'Immigrant Song', 'Spank Thru', 'Hairspray Queen', 'School' and 'Mr Moustache'.

This amateur home movie has since been released on a DVD included in the With The Lights Out package, and it is a fascinating record of the band's development. Most of Nirvana's fans worldwide are accustomed to their incendiary use of drama, contrast and timing, their spine-tingling dips and blazing outbursts, their compellingly eerie melodies - but they won't find any of that here.

In my own review of the film in British music magazine Classic Rock, I ventured that Nirvana at the Novoselic household could have been "any band in any bedroom anywhere, thrashing out bludgeoning, sub-Sabbath riffs, murdering Zeppelin and indulging a fleeting Beatles influence in 'About A Girl'. Krist Novoselic thought that 'It's kind of the bridge between grunge and pop right there.' A formidable combination, but back then they were too primitive to master it. Over the course of nine songs, their friends, lazing around on the floor, are naturally unaware that they are in the presence of greatness; that the wretched din they are cheering on will soon mutate into something wilder, but so dynamic and emotional..."

And then there was Kurt: "with his long, mousey hair and beat-up jeans, [he] scarcely shows his face, keeping his back to the camera as he bellows unintelligibly into a microphone placed at the opposite wall."

Not a particularly outstanding work then, but it was all about the raw power, the primal scream. Luckily, Jack Endino knew how to harness Nirvana's savagery, to make it more communicative without diluting the rage. This was his task when the band began recording their first album, provisionally titled Too Many Humans, on Christmas Eve 1988.

Everett True was the catalyst for what happened next. He was a rock writer and a truly emotional fan. He loved music that had meaningful, spontaneous, reckless spirit. He loved to dance and to revel in the mutual exchange of energy and the physical partnership of stage diving. In his guise as 'The Legend!' - preferably after much alcohol had been taken - he would gladly leap on to his own and anyone else's stage to perform lusty, minimalist versions of his favourite pop, punk and soul songs as well as some originals. He became a Sub Pop artist.

Perhaps a little like Cobain, True had a shy humility about him that could erupt at late moments of the evening into displays of extroverted and tumultuous excess. In time, he would make his reputation as the most comprehensive chronicler of Sub Pop, the Seattle scene and Nirvana, much of this for Melody Maker. He would become a trusted friend and confidante to Kurt Cobain and Courtney Love, and would go on to produce the most informed and personal biography that exists about Nirvana, The True Story.

No one could have predicted the reverberations from True's first visit to Seattle at the beginning of 1989, paid for by Sub Pop and organised by Anton Brookes, a publicist working for the label's UK distributor, Southern. (Brookes later set up his own PR agency, Bad Moon.) Sub Pop, as usual, did not have a lot of spare cash, but it seemed to Bruce Pavitt that he should seize the moment. The label had released the compilation set Sub Pop 200 at the end of 1988, featuring Nirvana's "Spank Thru", as well as tracks by Soundgarden, Mudhoney, Beat Happening, Green River, Screaming Trees, Tad and others - and the BBC's legendary radio presenter John Peel had started playing selections on his show.

The people of Seattle, a fairly isolated city geographically, had thought of their music scene as something that was cool and fun and unlikely to travel too far beyond their own state. It seemed scarcely credible that thousands of miles away, the UK was taking an interest.

When Anton Brookes informed Pavitt that Melody Maker was offering a cover story on Mudhoney followed by a feature about Sub Pop, he agreed to foot the bill. True flew to Seattle with photographer Andy Catlin, and stayed on a mattress at Pavitt's own home.

Pavitt later told Cynthia Rose, writing for Dazed & Confused, about True: "And he wrote a big, over-the-top, hype piece about

Seattle rock. And that did us a lot of good, 'cause, as we all know, if something starts getting big in the UK, then people here at home start respecting it more. We knew that the only way we could maybe break through was to use the British press. At the same time, we also released Sub Pop 200 and Peel was playing it. And he wrote a review - in the London Times - stating that the music was the most distinctive regional sound since Detroit's Motown. That in itself was quite an incredible statement. So we had this one-two punch: him and Melody Maker. And, I have to say, without that support from the UK, Sub Pop would probably have folded long ago."

Everett's article, published on March 18 1989 (with the second part to follow), used the word "grunge" for the first time anywhere to describe the sound of the music he heard in Seattle. He talked of "hordes of shit-kicking, life-defying, grungy, gory, guitar bands with one foot in the early Seventies and the other on punk rock's grave", giving particular mention to Tad's "spine-crushing band" and "the incredible Nirvana".

Unfortunately, Nirvana weren't that incredible when True first saw them playing live at the HUB Ballroom at the University of Washington on February 25 with Skin Yard, Girl Trouble and The Fluid.

"I was disappointed," he confided in The True Story. "I loved their single, but what was this mess of noise and hair and alcohol-fuelled banter?" He went on to complain that the music was a "formless compendium of noise for noise's sake, no pop tunes or spark or anything. Sure, they seemed like fun, mischievous folk: Krist in particular was determined to make an impression, whatever it took. Placed next to characters such as Tad Doyle and his gross, evil humour, though, this Aberdeen quartet paled into insignificance. They did destroy their instruments, though..."

Everett was not mistaken when he used the word "quartet".

Nirvana had just recruited a rhythm guitarist, Jason Everman, an old bandmate of Chad Channing's in Stone Crow, to beef up the sound and allow Cobain the space to concentrate on his lead lines and sonic experiments. John Troutman, a friend of Jason's, was also at the HUB gig. He told Carrie Borzillo: "Most of us were busy watching and listening to see what difference Jason made. And Jason just kicked up a hell of a racket. I can see why they were looking for something maybe like him, but I would also see why maybe he didn't last very long. Jason was into the most insane heavy metal you'd ever heard and he was a metal guitarist onstage too - all over the place and the hair was everywhere and he'd play power chords that were just huge and sustaining. It was a more full sound, but it was definitely sort of edging on too hard a guitar sound for them. It wasn't organic enough. It just wasn't quite right."

Borzillo also spoke about the HUB concert with The Posies' Mike Musburger who, having witnessed Nirvana, rushed back to tell the rest of his own group: "I just saw the greatest band." Where Everett True had heard no tunes, Musburger said he was astonished by Nirvana's blend of mayhem and melody. Of the gear-trashing, he added: "There was such a vengeance and violence to it that it seemed kind of comical also. It had this strange combination of scariness and comedy at the same time."

Charles Peterson, the Sub Pop photographer who'd been so desperately unimpressed by Nirvana's first gig at The Vogue, was happy to take their picture at the HUB Ballroom, announcing that, "They totally blew me away... they tore up the stage."

Nirvana fan Rob Kader told True what he, too, had enjoyed about the gig: "Just the intensity. The whole band, and Kurt in particular, played until they had nothing left. It was brutal, the way he put his body through so much."

Nevertheless, Everett True was adamant that Nirvana did not take the audience by storm that night. In his estimation, they were just one of the groups around a vibrant and exhilarating music scene in Seattle. His love affair with Nirvana would not yet flourish, although the publication of his article in Melody Maker set another ball in motion: from now on, Seattle would start feeling the heat of the media spotlight.

The band had ended 1988 by persuading Sub Pop to give them a contract. More accurately, a drunk and aggressive Krist Novoselic had lurched up to Bruce Pavitt's door and demanded one. The deal - for up to three albums - came into force on January 1, 1989. This was the first time Sub Pop had signed a group long-term. Satisfied that they'd put their career on to a more businesslike footing, the band recorded their debut album for Sub Pop.

They had to pay the studio costs themselves - $606.17 -, and they borrowed it from Chad's friend Jason Everman, who hadn't yet taken up his guitarist's position with Nirvana. Still, he was pictured and credited on the album sleeve by way of a thank you and a welcome, although he was not on the recordings. There were six sessions with Jack Endino at Reciprocal Recording, taking place between December 24 and January 24. The band would then spend most of 1989 on the road.

On January 6, they ventured out of Washington State for the first time to support the Dharma Bums at the Satyricon club in Portland, Oregon. This is thought to be the gig at which Courtney Love first saw Nirvana and her future second husband. If this is true and if she even met him on that occasion, it could only have been fleeting. It was Everett True who would later introduce Kurt and Courtney.

Nirvana jumped into Novoselic's van for their first tour away from home: a week in California opening for the Melvins and Mudhoney, beginning on February 10. This was where Jason Everman came in, finding his feet in the band without undue pressure in a place where nobody really knew them.

Their second gig, at Palo Alto, was where guitarist Steve Turner from headliners Mudhoney saw something vividly memorable, something he, and others, have described to various biographers. Turner told Everett True: "And Kurt was rolling around on the stage and he kind of rolled backwards and somehow managed to be balancing on his head and still playing his guitar - it was the weirdest thing because he was like magically balancing on his head without using his hands".

In the spring, back in Olympia, Nirvana made a tape with student Greg Babior, who was compiling a project for the Evergreen State College in that establishment's studio. It offered 16- or 24-track recording - a step up from Endino's eight. Greg, who later played in Earth, remembered Nirvana charging quite spontaneously through a cover of Kiss's 'Do You Love Me?' (later released on a C/Z Kiss tribute album) but taking time over their own song, 'Dive', a recording subsequently issued on With The Lights Out. Babior noticed that Jason Everman had trouble with his guitar parts. Already, there were signs that for all of his wild curly hair and onstage mania, Everman was not fully tuned into Nirvana.

They continued to tour through to the early summer. The further they ventured from home ground, the more uncertain their reception. However, although they were poorly received in California and Oregon, the tour was saved when they returned to Seattle, playing to a crowd of 600 people at the University of Washington. This was one occasion on which Nirvana's music and performance style was perfectly suited to the mood of the young people who were listening. As the band played, the audience went wild, crashing into each other and climbing onto the stage, only to hurl themselves back into the seething pit they had just emerged from. Nirvana's angry, powerful music spoke of the way modern living was ignoring their personal desires, and it tempted the crowd to act. This they did by throwing themselves around, wreaking havoc on their surroundings. If the world needed a sign that grunge was the music for a disillusioned youth, this was it.

However, on April 7, at the Annex Theatre in Seattle, Nirvana notched up another first with Kurt Cobain being held aloft by the audience - a hero's honour. They went down equally well on a bill with Flaming Lips at The Vogue where, according to one writer, "There was a lot of shit getting trashed, people throwing stuff everywhere...the buzz was really starting to grow on Nirvana."

Flaming Lips frontman Wayne Coyne had been unconvinced by Jonathan Poneman's proclamations that Nirvana would be the band to bring glory to Sub Pop and Seattle. Coyne thought their music erred too much towards bad thrash metal, but he would later hear great riffs and melodies emerging, and he would come to appreciate the perversity of Cobain, who dared to look like a hippie with his long, straggly hair and unshaven chin.

Coyne told Carrie Borzillo: "Everyone talked about the fusion of classic rock and punk rock - you could walk away singing, 'I'm a negative creep! I'm a negative creep!' In the end, it just floored us."

Nirvana put it like this in an official Sub Pop press release: "Nirvana sounds like mid-tempo Black Sabbath playing The Knack, Black Flag, the Stooges and a pinch of the Bay City Rollers."

Another convert was Screaming Trees' Mark Lanegan, who later told Spin magazine: "They completely blew me away. It was like seeing The Who in their prime. After two songs some jerk who worked there stopped the show - they'd gone over their time limit. So they stood there for a second and then Krist started throwing his bass up in the air, up to the top of this 20-foot ceiling, and catching it with one hand. Meanwhile, Kurt was letting his amp go loud as hell, and their road manager got in a fist-fight with the jerk guy. And this was in Ellensburg!"

On June 9, Nirvana appeared with Tad, Mudhoney and Blood Circus at the Sub Pop Lame Fest, held at Seattle's Moore Theatre, where they created pandemonium, slaying their biggest audience to date. Joe Newton, drummer with a band called Gas Huffer, told Everett True: "They had this abandon that rock'n'roll is supposed to have, this 'rolling in glass' kind of thing. It was just the ability to let go of your mortality, to not fear getting injured."

Six days later, their debut album, now known as Bleach because while on tour the band had seen an AIDS prevention poster which advised heroin users to bleach their needles before use, was unleashed upon an unsuspecting United States. It would be released in the UK in August.

CHAPTER 4

Sub Pop hoped to sell a few thousand copies of this convincing but hardly commercial collection from Nirvana. Predominantly noisy, dark and doomy, slow and sludgy, heavy on the bass and fuzz, and lit by shafts of tunefulness, it's a bitterly angry, brooding and intense work that offers relief onlyin the semi-acoustic poppiness of one track, 'About A Girl'.

Cobain had penned 'About A Girl' during a prolific burst of song writing at his Olympia flat in the spring of 1988. It was all about the state of his relationship with Tracy Marander, back when she was working nights, leaving lists of household duties for him to carry out.

'School' transposed the cliquey mentality of the school playground to that of adults in the real world and particularly the Sub Pop circles of Seattle, while 'Paper Cuts' referred to a genuine family in Aberdeen who kept their children locked up in one room in disgusting conditions.

Chad Channing said to Everett True: "They were mostly songs about lower life society... and there were some campy things like 'Floyd The Barber'."

Kurt Cobain later confessed to Spin magazine: "With Bleach, I didn't give a flying fuck what the lyrics were about. Eighty per cent were written the night before recording. It was like, 'I'm pissed off. Don't know what about. Let's just scream negative lyrics and as long as they're not sexist and don't get too embarrassing it'll be okay.' I don't hold any of those lyrics dear to me."

Asked about the "rawness" and "heaviness" of the album, he told Carl Williams from Metal Forces magazine: "I think a lot of music today sounds far too polished, there's no energy. It's too programmed and fake, you hear too much. I want a little mud in my music."

In 1992, Cobain said in Nevermind: It's An Interview: "Bleach seemed to be really one-dimensional. It has the same format throughout - there were a few guitar overdubs, but that's it. All the songs are slow and grungy and they're tuned down to really low notes. And I screamed a lot. But at the same time that we were recording, we had a lot more songs like 'About A Girl'. In fact, 'Polly' was written at that time too. It's just that we chose to put more abrasive songs on the Bleach album."

There was a reason for this, as Kurt explained to Michael Azerrad: "We purposely made Bleach one-dimensional, more 'rock' than it should have been. There was this pressure from Sub Pop and the scene to play 'rock music', strip it down and make it sound like Aerosmith."

Bleach, which happily sounded nothing like Aerosmith, didn't chart on either side of the Atlantic, but it was greeted with excitement by some sections of the indie and rock press, the local papers and the band's long-standing champions. Gillian G. Gaar informed readers of the Rocket: "Nirvana careers from one end of the thrash spectrum to the other, giving a nod towards garage, grunge, alternative noise and hell-raising metal without swearing allegiance to any of them."

Guitar World later described Bleach as "an intensely physical melange of un-tuned metal, drunk punk, and Seventies pop, written from the perspective of a college drop-out," while in Rolling Stone's Ira Robbins' assessment, it was "undistinguished" and "relied on warmed-over Seventies metal riffs".

The Posies' Mike Musburger picked up on the band's increasing tunefulness, telling Carrie Borzillo: "The whole idea of the loud/soft distorted guitars and the really chunky guitars, I'd already heard that... But Nirvana was the first band that really took that idea and wrote pop songs with it."

The album included three tracks recorded during the January 1988 demo sessions with Dale Crover - 'Floyd The Barber', 'Paper Cuts' and 'Downer. It was decided that since Dale had created those drum parts in the first place, he naturally played them better than anyone else.

On June 21, Nirvana played a farewell gig in Seattle, at The Vogue, before hitting the road in Krist's van for their first full US tour. It began in California, where Nirvana opened in San Francisco and improved slightly on their previous audience numbers. They carried on with gigs in Westwood, LA and Long Beach before driving hundreds of miles to play support gigs to a couple of dozen punters in states they'd never seen before: New Mexico, Texas - where they famously slept out in a wood armed with baseball bats for fear of being disturbed by the native alligators, Minnesota, Illinois, Wisconsin, Pennsylvania, New Jersey, Massachusetts and finally, New York. The band had been booked for an appearance with Tad at the state capital's Pyramid Club as part of the New Music Seminar.

As Kurt fondly reminisced, "We chose to tour in the middle of the summer," he laughed. "In the South - imagine being in Texas in July, packed up to the rim of the van with T-shirts and equipment, with four members, with no air conditioning, tooling around, living on $30 a day if you're lucky. It was fun but we should have been a little smarter about it. We should have toured in September or something, but we were so excited about getting the record out and going on tour that we just went for it."

John Robb, journalist and esteemed punk singer, attended two shows for a cover story in the British music weekly Sounds, a gig at Maxwell's in Hoboken, NJ, and the Pyramid Club. He later recalled, in The True Story, "I loved Kurt's voice. It sounded old and weary, yet wild and free, a cracked rough gnarl of a voice, a voice that sounded like it had screamed hard

down the mic many times - it cut right through. I dug the band's primal, feral bestiality and the way on their first single they'd taken Shocking Blue's original and turned it into a fierce blast of teen alienation."

Anton Brookes, Nirvana's press representative in the UK, was also seeing the band for the first time at these shows. He told True that it was only then he understood Jonathan Poneman's evangelical enthusiasm: "Because within this rage, this tornado, there was a subtlety and a tenderness. Nirvana's songs were ugly-beautiful."

Janet Billig, looking after promotion and publicity for Sub Pop artists touring the East Coast, caught Nirvana in Massachusetts, later telling Everett True that "there was something magical about Kurt" and asserting: "It was like watching a rolling ball of fire that kept getting stronger and stronger."

There were dissenting voices. Outside of Washington, Nirvana drew extreme reactions from those who saw them. Various witnesses at the Pyramid show have said it was pretty awful. For the main part, though, the band made friends and influenced people, building on the buzz created by the media coverage, 'Love Buzz' and Bleach.

New York was not supposed to have been the concluding tour date. They were due to go to Canada next, but they suddenly abandoned the itinerary and drove back to Washington.

Jason Everman had been getting more and more withdrawn as the tour progressed. Unspoken tensions had been building. Everman is thought to have felt excluded by the close friendship between Cobain and Novoselic and by the fact that they were the decision-makers in the band. He felt that his opinions counted for nothing; nor, for that matter, did Chad's. On the other hand, Kurt and Krist resented the atmosphere that Everman's sulky silences were creating, and they were instinctively starting to agree with the criticisms of various supporters who'd felt from the outset that Jason was too much of a heavy metal player and too much of a rock poser for Nirvana.

Sadly for his friend Chad Channing, Kurt and Krist decided to release Jason. Instead of telling him this, they simply cut short the tour and headed homewards - a long and uncomfortable drive in which no one expressed their feelings. Everman was now Nirvana's ex- rhythm guitarist. He just didn't know it yet. He would next team up with Soundgarden - still at that time the biggest band in Seattle - playing bass. Later replaced by Ben Shepherd, he would return to the guitar to join Mindfunk.

Nirvana were to continue as a three-piece band for the foreseeable future.

For some undisclosed reason, they gave Jack Endino a miss when they next went into the studio. In August, they repaired to Music Source, a 24-track facility, where Steve Fisk produced two new tracks for the Blew EP. Fisk had previously thought Nirvana's music execrable and had walked out of their April gig at Ellensburg - the show that had so impressed Mark Lanegan. Now, Fisk - an alternative musician himself - had reassessed the band and was thoroughly excited to be working with them.

They taped 'Been A Son', a song about Don Cobain's disappointment that Kurt's sibling, Kim, had been born a girl and not a boy, and 'Stain', which also arose from the troubled family past. Both songs appeared on the EP. Also recorded but not finished were a trio that have since been issued on With The Lights Out: 'Token Eastern Song', 'Even In His Youth' and the anti-rape song 'Polly' - a dramatic story triggered by the real-life kidnap, rape and torture of a 14-year-old girl in Tacoma in June 1987.

Cobain later explained to Hits magazine: "It's a story about a rapist who captures a sadomasochist and this woman, 'Polly', is having sex as a way to develop a relationship. He rapes her at first and they have a relationship and they fall in love, then eventually she kills him and runs away... I just thought that a standard song about rape would be boring and trite."

Another significant project in August involved Kurt, Krist and Screaming Trees' Mark Lanegan and Mark Pickerel, their drummer. Kurt and Mark had recently written a batch of songs together and they intended to record them for an album under the name of The Jury. Turning up at Reciprocal Recording with Novoselic and Pickerel, they eventually confessed to Jack Endino that they couldn't remember the songs. They decided not to waste the studio time - on August 20 and 28 - and instead turned in a handful of covers. These were all songs by Leadbelly, the influential black folk-blues singer and guitarist.

Four tracks were completed and they were full of feeling, the musicians wholly absorbed in an old musical tradition to which they brought contemporary meaning. 'Where Did You Sleep Last Night' later appeared on Lanegan's first solo album, The Winding Sheet, the next year, and would also become a familiar feature of Nirvana's set. The other songs, 'They Hung Him On The Cross', 'Grey Goose' and 'Ain't It A Shame', were finally made public on With The Lights Out. Of all 81 tracks on the collection, these are arguably the most fascinating. Kurt sings the blues, as you'd expect, with soul, and as you wouldn't expect, with an exceptional and sometimes mature versatility.

Nirvana spent the summer months playing around Washington State, only occasionally performing in Seattle where their shows now sold out easily. This didn't mean that they were naturally welcomed into the city's tight musical community. On the contrary, they were still regarded as outsiders, albeit outsiders that everyone wanted to see.

Things were on the up. When the band departed Seattle in September 1989 for a string of dates in the Mid-West, making up for some of the cancelled gigs on their earlier, truncated tour with Jason Everman, they enjoyed the luxury of an informal road manager - their friend Ben Shepherd, who made himself useful in return for his free ticket; a sound engineer, Craig Montgomery; and a truck for their equipment. On a decent night, Nirvana could pull a crowd of 200 and command between $100 and $200 per gig.

Towards the end of October, they travelled to Europe, co-headlining the aptly named "Heavier Than Heaven" tour with Tad, and the insanity they unlocked in the audiences there was unlike anything they'd ever experienced.

In 1989 there was a drought of quality rock acts throughout Europe. The British charts were filled with pre-packaged pop music, with the likes of Stock, Aitken and Waterman churning out hits for a stream of clean-cut, well turned out, unspeakably bad singers to sing, and there was precious little for a fan of either punk or rock to listen to in the mainstream. Radio 1 DJ John Peel was championing the underground cause, and anyone who wanted to hear something other than reconstituted Kylie and Jason could tune in to his show; but his was an island in a sea of banality.

This dearth wasn't for want of an audience. The UK had a long history of rock fans, and, as was to be proven in the coming years, they were certainly receptive to the kind of music Nirvana and the other Northwest bands were producing. There seemed to be no reason for this vacuum; it was just an example of one of those occasions where there was a need for something that didn't yet exist. In a situation like this, demand drives the market, and as soon as a record company realises there is space to monopolise in this void, they can make a killing.

Into this climate came bands from the Northwest US, ready to alleviate the boredom inspired by 80s pop music. People throughout the country had been waiting for something, new acts, to break the hold this pop had on the charts and on the mainstream radio stations; and when it eventually came, there

was huge support for these acts. Nirvana was to find one of its most faithful fan bases in the UK, and they would reward them with some of their best live performances.

Kurt remembered those times as being hard, yet a lot of fun, and he seemed happiest and most comfortable with the band's less-than-lofty position. "Being in Europe for the first time was more romantic," he remembered. "It wasn't any more comfortable. We were living off of deli trays and cigarettes. And bad beer, or strong beer, I should say. I guess you would call that good beer, wouldn't you? I don't like beer. There were 11 people in a small Euro van. The seats were at this angle, so you would try to sleep and we'd be on like 15-to-18-hour drives just crammed up against one another. And all in the dead of winter. It was fun, but after seven weeks it took its toll on everyone."

They were ushered into the UK with another of Everett True's Melody Maker features, this one titled "Bleached Wails", in which he talked to the band about the Seattle and Sub Pop phenomenon, and the accusations of hype. Nirvana lined up alongside people like Iggy Pop and The Stooges, bands who ran on spontaneity and adrenalin. They insisted that they would be playing precisely the same music whatever the prevailing musical climate in Washington.

The tour began in high spirits, although in many ways, it became a huge ordeal. The two bands were jammed together in a mini-van with Craig Montgomery, a Dutch tour manager called Edwin Heath and their gear. That didn't allow for a lot of room, given the enormous girth of Tad Doyle and the 6' 7" frame of Krist Novoselic. There was a great deal of driving involved. The band was scheduled to play 37 dates in 42 days, sometimes having to set off immediately after a show for an overnight drive to the next. It was a cold, wet autumn, too.

There were niggles between the bands. Although they had

been friendly back in Washington, the claustrophobia of the van and the enforced proximity of its occupants gave rise to irritations. The Tad contingent was particularly annoyed by Nirvana's insistence on trashing shared equipment.

Outside of London, the gigs were modest, taking place in pubs, student halls or small theatres. They weren't all sold out, but the people who did turn out for the gigs were those who knew all about the bands arriving on these shores for the first time. These were ground-breaking shows; a launch pad. A lot of record-company A&R folk had travelled to the regional gigs to see Nirvana before they arrived in London.

Things got off to a bad start on the first night, at a packed Newcastle Riverside on October 23, when problems arose with the rented equipment, including the drum kit. Chad Channing remembers someone in the crowd lobbing a beer bottle straight at Krist Novoselic's head. Craig Montgomery recalled a drunken Novoselic trashing a bass amplifier.

Things improved. In Manchester, there was mania. In Leeds, the Duchess of York sizzled. In London, at the School of Oriental and African Studies on October 27, the fans went berserk, slam-dancing, leaping off speaker stacks and rushing the stage. It was the wildest reception of Nirvana's career so far, but one to which they soon would become accustomed.

"I'd never seen anything like it," Montgomery told Carrie Borzillo. "I ended up seeing it with Nirvana all the time, though. They would play this stuff and it was like a tornado hit. People would completely lose control of their bodies."

Carl Williams, interviewing the band backstage at the gig for the UK's Metal Forces magazine, declared that Nirvana were "probably the best new band this year", adding: "For the first time in years something highly original is sweeping the musical world and at the forefront of this wave of new talent is NIRVANA, a Seattle based band... who embody the rule-breaking aspect of things, right down to their 'image', or, to be more precise, their total absence of image."

They talked a lot about Aberdeen, where "everyone was so negative and macho all the time," according to Kurt, and about 'Negative Creep', the audiences' favourite song.

Come November 1, Nirvana and Tad had arrived in Holland, the home of their booking agency Paperclip. Here the venues were larger and the hospitality exemplary. In Amsterdam, the musicians had fun investigating the legal hash bars. At the gigs, though, according to Montgomery, "Audiences were a little more reserved... They weren't going nuts like the English."

On to Germany, and the bands had the privilege to witness history in the making when the Berlin Wall fell on November 9. That day they were in Hanover. Two nights later, having gasped at the miles-long queue of cars heading from the east into the west, they played in the previously divided city, which was still partying. Kurt, however, was not in a jubilant mood onstage. He'd been wrecking his guitars and repairing them after a fashion, but his sound was getting progressively worse. In Berlin's Ecstasy Club, he gave up in disgust, smashed his instrument and stormed off stage before the end of the set.

The tour rattled on through Austria, Switzerland and Italy where in Rome, at the Piper Club on November 27, Cobain threw a distinctly dangerous strop. Furious about the monitors and yet again about his guitar sound, homesick and exhausted, he scaled the PA stack, teetered on the edge, and threatened to jump. From there, he climbed on to the rafters and then appeared on the balcony, swearing he would hurl chairs down on to the "morons" in the auditorium. Every member of Nirvana vowed to leave the band that night, as did their manager Heath, who had never encountered such reckless disregard for life, limb - and equipment.

Bruce Pavitt and Jonathan Poneman had flown over for the

Rome gig in a show of support for Tad and Nirvana. Poneman sought to calm the troubled waters by promising Kurt a new guitar when the tour returned to Switzerland, the next destination, and arranging for him to travel there by train with himself and Pavitt, just to escape the maddening confines of the van. The label men had to do everything in their power to safeguard the tour since it was due to culminate in a big Sub Pop celebration in London in only a few days' time. It coincided with the release of the Blew EP.

Kurt later told Guitar World's Jon Savage that "by the seventh week [of the tour], I was ready to die."

Cobain's mood blackened when, travelling from Rome to Geneva on the train, someone stole his wallet and passport. Much red tape later, Nirvana appeared as planned in Geneva and Zurich, France and Belgium, before arriving in England - much to everyone's relief - on December 3 for Sub Pop's Lame Fest at the London Astoria.

Tad and Nirvana shared the bill with Mudhoney, who were also touring Europe, and Nirvana were elected, at the flip of a coin, to go on first. At this prestigious London gig, they gave a ferocious performance in which they inspired flurries of stage diving, played baseball with their guitars, smashed up equipment and divided opinion in their usual extreme manner. Fellow musicians, journalists and music industry individuals decided they were either brilliant or a terrible flop.

Everett True, who up to this point had preferred Soundgarden and Mudhoney, says in The True Story that at the Astoria, "Nirvana totally tore up the rulebook. This, in many respects, was the show that changed everything."

He adds: "After 30 minutes, they'd pulverised their way through four guitars and left the stage for dead... I'm sure this is the night that I first really connected with the power and rage and frustration and sheer devilment of Kurt Cobain."

Melody Maker photographer Stephen Sweet agreed with True, stating: "Kurt was in turn full of terror and gentleness. He threw himself around like nothing existed outside of each moment he played and sang."

Christof Ellinghaus, their German booking agent, commented: "Nirvana stole the show. They were a menace, amazing."

Anton Brookes recalls in The True Story: "That night was the turning point. There were a lot of hipsters there, the cool bands - Kurt came off stage and his knees were all cut up and grazed because he'd jump four or five feet in the air off something and land on his knees... I thought it was really good. The following week all the reviews made Nirvana out to be the band. I felt sorry for Mudhoney because I thought they were amazing... but it was Nirvana getting the accolades."

Not everyone turned in awestruck reviews. True's Melody Maker colleague Simon Price complained that Novoselic's buffoonery ruined the gig. And as for Mudhoney - they were scandalised. Drummer Dan Peters told True that Nirvana were "fucking horrible" and "fucking shitty", adding: "They could barely get through a song, let alone 10 songs. They were breaking strings left and right. At one point Krist was swinging his bass around and I was standing on the side of the stage. All of a sudden it got loose and I fucking had to put my hand up and the butt of his bass hit me. If I'd been any slower..."

Novoselic later said that he thought the show "stunk", rating it nought out of 10, although two songs clearly passed the acid test: these versions of 'Polly' and 'Breed' were later released on the posthumous Nirvana album, From The Muddy Banks of the Wishkah.

This European tour, and the Lame Fest in particular, undeniably opened the doors for Nirvana, increasing their profile and astonishing many fans who now formed the core of a rapidly mushrooming following.

Everett True, who saw every gig on the tour, gathers his thoughts in The True Story: "All I can recollect is long hair and faces insane on alcohol and heat, body aching from constant dancing, head spinning from resting it within the bass drums... There must have come a time when Nirvana went from being a second-rate Soundgarden to an incredible, emotionally charged live act and it must have happened on this tour... Nirvana had so much angst to get out of their scrawny systems."

"That's also why Kurt started leaping backwards into the drum kit, forwards into the crowd, like Nick Cave and Iggy Pop before him. And that's why I loved Nirvana so much initially. They made a goddam effort - by leaping around and gurning and groaning and screaming so much on stage. Put your heart and soul and body into it because you know what? Outside of tonight, nothing exists."

From now on True would become Nirvana's most trusted chronicler, although this had its pitfalls. While other journalists had certainly come on board, including John Robb and Keith Cameron, both True and Melody Maker would become so inextricably linked to Sub Pop and Nirvana that the rival music press was unwilling to be seen to be toeing the line. Largely, they reserved judgement until Nirvana became absolutely undeniable.

On December 30, 1989, Krist Novoselic married Shelli in Tacoma, Washington, with old pal Mudhoney's Matt Lukin carrying out best man duties.

More and more people were starting to get it. Nirvana may have found their European tour draining, but early in January 1990, they were back on the road in Seattle, Portland, Olympia and Tacoma, where Seaweed singer Aaron Stauffer caught the show. He later told Everett True that, on this occasion "for the first and only time I thought Nirvana were better than Melvins". The headline act was noticeably less well attended than the

support, and those who had come to see Nirvana included several members of Mudhoney, most notably Mark Arm. As part of Green River, he had begun the grunge movement, and as the leader of Mudhoney was at the forefront of the fight to make grunge heard around the world. The very fact that Arm and the rest of his band were there watching, dancing and clearly enjoying themselves was a sign that Nirvana had been accepted as a member of the revolution. The band was beginning to surpass its mentors.

As Nirvana received a much better reception than the Melvins, it was obvious the younger band had moved on. They no longer lived and performed in the shadow of Aberdeen's biggest band. Nirvana was quickly becoming Aberdeen's biggest band. They were a unique and powerful band in their own right, and now they would start proving this to the world.

At this stage, Kurt and co still exhibited a juvenile sense of humour and fun - many people who met Cobain noted a child-like wonder and naivety about him - which balanced the band's collective passion and intensity and, also, an unintended sexual allure. They abhorred the archetypal rock-star treatment of female fans and were vocal in their support of women in society and in music.

In February, Nirvana once set out with Tad on a string of West Coast dates. They caused a sensation on February 15 at Raji's in LA, where Cobain repeatedly flung himself into the drum kit and was memorably photographed by Charles Peterson plunging backwards into flying snares and toms. In Tijuana, San Diego radio DJ Dave Lott was left reeling by Kurt's performance. Lott told Carrie Borzillo: "Just to look at him and hear that was like, that sound is coming out of him? When he left the stage, everyone stood there kind of dazed."

Everett True flew out to cover the tour for Melody Maker. He reported that, "Right now... Nirvana are awesome live."

Describing the show at San Francisco's Kennel Club on Valentine's Day, he wrote: "The Washington trio blow every other fucking band in existence off-centre with their potency and ferocious intent. 'Love Buzz' and 'Stain' spiral and shatter, leaving precious shards of the purest pop thrill in their wake."

On April Fool's Day, Nirvana began yet another US tour in Chicago. Chicago Tribune reviewer Greg Kot told Carrie Borzillo: "I'll never forget what I saw that night. It was like, 'Oh my God - Nirvana are amazing.'"

By now, Kurt's hair was blond, a fact reported by Kot who seemed surprised that Cobain was "screaming his guts out" for the duration of the set. Kot added: "He looked like he was in the jaws of this giant invisible Rottweiler and the Rottweiler was just shaking him back and forth... This scrawny little guy was just flinging his body around the stage with absolutely no regard for the consequences." After a spectacular smashing-up of their instruments, they walked off leaving local band Eleventh Dream Day with no chance of triumph on their own turf.

In the morning, Nirvana took a five-day break to go into producer Butch Vig's Smart Studios in Madison, Wisconsin. The material they completed there was intended for their next Sub Pop album. As it turned out, the recordings would end up as demos for their world-conquering major-label debut, Nevermind. Five songs would make it on to the album: 'In Bloom', 'Lithium', 'Stay Away' (then called 'Pay To Play'), 'Breed' ('Imodium') and 'Polly'. The version of 'Polly' was the only track from these sessions that would be used on Nevermind, albeit with overdubs. The band also taped a Velvet Underground song, 'Here She Comes Now'. This cover was released on a VU tribute album, Heaven And Hell Vol 1 and also, years later, on With The Lights Out, along with 'Pay To Play'.

Vig - later a successful pop-chart musician in his own right with the "superband" Garbage - in these earlier days specialised in alternative rock acts such as Tad, Killdozer and The Fluid. But he hadn't been a massive fan of Nirvana: the only track from Bleach that had really impressed him was their gentlest, 'About A Girl'. Now he was confronted with a band who was demanding a heavy-monster production, and yet he could see lightness, tunefulness, in the songs they were bringing to his studio.

He recollected: "The thing that I noticed right off the bat was that Kurt wrote amazing songs and Krist wrote super hooky bass lines. The bass lines are really melodic, and the hook under the song was actually in the bass, at least musically. And that works so well with Kurt's vocal melody. They had a really cool interweaving quality."

The session would lead to the band becoming enamoured with Butch Vig, who had managed to capture the Nirvana sound in a way that was honest and representative of their live performances, whilst at the same time opening it up, accentuating their strong song writing. Vig and Nirvana would record together again for the album, and this mutual respect and understanding would form the basis of Nevermind's success. Vig knew how to transfer Nirvana's massive sound onto a record that would be played in someone's bedroom, which was exactly what the band wanted.

Vig saw his first live Nirvana show on April 6, at a venue in Madison. "It was a great set, very loose," he later recalled.

These were the last recordings that Chad Channing made with Nirvana. Chad had been the only member of the band to keep smiling throughout the gruelling European tour, but now he was starting to resent his role as a "drum machine". He was eager to contribute ideas to the music - he claims, with Cobain's encouragement - but with the Butch Vig sessions, he realised it wasn't going to happen. The band was ruled by the partnership of Cobain and Novoselic. Channing's disillusionment started to show in his performances.

Butch Vig noticed the tension. He said in a Goldmine interview: "I could tell that Kurt wasn't too pleased with Chad's drumming because he kept going and getting behind the kit showing him how to play things."

It was almost, but not quite, the end of the line for Chad - and also for Kurt's girlfriend Tracy Marander, whom he dumped in a phone call towards the end of April. Secretly, Kurt had fallen in love with one of Tracy's friends, Tobi Vail, who had known him in the days when he hung out with the Melvins. Tobi went on to start a fanzine, Jigsaw, start the Riot Grrrl movement - a punk-rock precursor to Girl Power - and become a founder member of Olympia hardcore band Bikini Kill.

Nirvana continued touring, winning new fans and attracting more press coverage with a set that by now included the songs they'd recorded with Vig. Gary Graff, a Detroit Free Press reporter, saw the show in Ann Arbor, Michigan, and he was aware of an almost tangible buzz around the group, a feeling that something big was about to happen. Nirvana responded with their usual charm offensive: "They had that total, 'Fuck you, we're gonna rock you. Deal with it' attitude," said Kurt St. Thomas, a radio station music director who would later question the band for Nevermind: It's An Interview. "But it seemed totally real. There was not one ounce of fake anything. It came off very sincere."

The air of expectancy was especially vivid in New York where Nirvana appeared at the Pyramid Club on April 26 with an audience including their own great hero Iggy Pop. Iggy had just been introduced to Sub Pop music and he judged Nirvana the best of the bands he'd heard. Also present were members of Sonic Youth and Helmet and, significantly, Gary Gersh, head of A&R at Geffen. Helmet's Page Hamilton thought that they were

shoddy and merely playing to the cameras (filming for a Sub Pop compilation) when they trashed the drum kit. The majority of the audience, however, thought they were sensational, with Janet Billig later proclaiming to Everett True that they "took over NYC". Novoselic however thought the show was so bad and such an embarrassment – and in front of punk hero Iggy Pop - that he punished himself severely: he shaved his head.

The tour wound up on May 17 at Boise, Idaho. Generally, it had been successful, although there had been one or two off nights. The band had also been troubled to hear from fans that they couldn't find Bleach in their local record stores, and Kurt's break-up with Tracy had soured his mood for a day or two. At the same time, Nirvana's reputation was growing, and their fees were rising at the same rate – they were now earning anywhere between $500 and $1,000 a night.

Kurt remarked to interviewer Bob Gulla that he was happy with the level of success they'd achieved; just a little more financial security would be perfect. His only real concern for the future, as the tour ended, was that he had to find a new drummer.

Cobain and Novoselic turned up at Chad Channing's door one day about a week later and fired him. Channing reacted with mixed emotions, but mainly relief. They announced the change in line up in typical fashion.

"Chad isn't in the band any more. We'll miss him. We will have a single out real soon. We recorded with Butch Vig in Madison. What a swell guy. We don't know what may lie ahead. Maybe we'll sign with Disney. Maybe we'll get a drum machine, maybe we'll get Phil Collins on drums. As for now, the politburo of Krist and Kurt bid you farewell."

CHAPTER 5

In fact, the A-side of the single that Nirvana released Stateside in September 1990 was not a Butch Vig recording. 'Sliver' - an ingenious slice of pop-noise - was produced and mixed by Jack Endino at Reciprocal Recording in July, and it featured Mudhoney drummer Dan Peters. Peters' opinion of the band had mellowed since his scathing appraisal of their performance at the London Astoria in December 1989, and he'd fallen for the Blew EP. 'Sliver's B-side - 'Dive' - was from the Vig sessions.

Before this, though, Nirvana had been doing a bit of shopping. They were unhappy with Sub Pop's precarious finances. Kurt and Krist also felt that Bleach could have been better distributed. They wanted a record company with enough clout to push their career as far as it could go while still respecting their alternative ideals.

They sought advice from Soundgarden's manager, Susan Silver. By now, Sub Pop and Seattle were big news, and almost every major label in the land was watching Nirvana. Silver introduced them to LA lawyer Alan Mintz, and he sent copies of the band's Butch Vig tapes to all of the leading players in the industry. Nirvana did not inform either Pavitt or Poneman that any of this was happening. As far as P&P were concerned, Nirvana were preparing their second album for release on Sub Pop. But rumours soon started getting back to Seattle: Nirvana and their friends were being courted, wined and dined on corporate expense accounts and, horror of horrors, they were swanning round Olympia in limousines.

This was a devastating blow to Pavitt and Poneman, mainly because Nirvana were going about things so secretively. The Sub Pop partners felt betrayed. Of course, there was a certain ideological disappointment. They'd been trying to build an ethical, independent community, one that depended on mutual trust and co-operation that could exist and prosper outside of the capitalist mainstream. They were even going so far as to talk to the "enemy" about distribution, just to be able to take the dream forward. Already, Soundgarden had gone to A&M and Sonic Youth to Geffen, but Nirvana's potential defection was heartbreaking for Pavitt and Poneman because it undermined their personal relationships with the band. While fully accepting that they didn't have the know-how or the bank account to deliver Nirvana to worldwide audiences, the partners believed they'd done their very best to support and nurture the band. To be dumped now - and, crucially, not to be told about it - was to have the hand of friendship bitten off.

In August, Nirvana played a short West Coast tour supporting Sonic Youth. Before it began, they spent a few days in San Francisco, staying with Melvin Buzz Osborne. It was at Osborne's suggestion that they went to see Washington, DC punk band Scream playing at the I Beam. Kurt was struck by the drummer, Dave Grohl: he would be perfect for Nirvana. Grohl's playing was very hard and heavy but it was solid, reliable, and as a bonus, he could sing great backing vocals. Cobain hoped that somewhere along the line, he would be able to grab Grohl.

In the meantime, Nirvana asked Dale Crover to drum for the tour, which opened on August 13 in Long Beach, California. Everywhere, it was obvious that things were stepping up a gear.

Carrie Borzillo spoke to several people who saw Nirvana at this time. Flipside fanzine writer Drunk Ted said of the San Diego gig: "This is one of the best shows I've ever seen. The Sub Pop thing was really happening and it was packed. Back then, Sub Poppers were known for having long hair and playing punkish garage music that was authentic. And it was really weird, 'cause when Nirvana showed up, Krist and Kurt had completely short

hair. Watching these guys play this totally twisted, hard music with short hair was strange. It was cool, though, 'cause they pulled it off. The show was so amazing. Nothing could compare to it." Posies drummer Mike Musburger, who saw the band in San Francisco, remarked: "I was really blown away. I think this was one of the first times I had an inkling that something bigger was going to happen."

Sub Pop's Megan Jasper told Borzillo about the Vancouver date: "This performance wowed me far more than any other Nirvana show. That was the night when, for me, they sort of crossed the line and went from this great local rock band to becoming something more. That was the time I really saw the doors open and I thought, 'My God. These guys really could be huge.'"

Sonic Youth all considered their support band amazing. Kim Gordon danced frenziedly throughout their set in Vegas. Lee Ranaldo said they were "incredibly exciting". And Thurston Moore told everyone who would listen how great they were. One of those who listened was Gold Mountain management boss Danny Goldberg. Gold Mountain's John Silva personally managed Sonic Youth, and Silva also came back off the road with fantastic reports of Nirvana. Within a couple of months, the band would have signed to Gold Mountain, encouraged by the fact that the company had the trust of Sonic Youth.

Back in Washington, Nirvana recruited Mudhoney's Dan Peters to join them on drums for a 15,000-capacity concert at the Motor Sports Arena alongside the Melvins, Dwarves and The Derelicts, on September 22. It was one of their most exciting performances to date. Susie Tennant, who worked for Geffen's DGC label in the Northwest, commented to Borzillo: "You just knew you were witnessing something. There was this feeling that everything was so amazing. Everyone knew that something big was gonna happen." Charles R Cross added: "Things started going crazy for them after this show, and suddenly they were bigger than Mudhoney. At that point, things shifted."

Dan Peters was thrilled; he believed he'd joined Nirvana. Indeed, he was photographed and interviewed with the band the next day for rock newspaper Sounds. Behind the scenes, however, Kurt and Krist were hard at work securing the services of Dave Grohl, who phoned to say that Scream had split and he'd heard from Buzz Osborne they needed a drummer. They invited Dave to Seattle to try out, even though they'd already engaged Dan Peters. Dave was in the crowd to see Nirvana's triumph at the Motor Sports Arena, and he later auditioned for the band. What he played was what Kurt and Krist wanted to hear. They further bonded over their mutual love of the Melvins, and Dave was in.

Kurt declared, "Its Dave who really brings the physicality to the dynamics in our songs," adding, "He's really good at copying other drummers' styles. He's got his own original style, too, but he also can play a Led Zeppelin solo note for note perfectly. You wouldn't be able to tell the difference. He's a great drummer. Dave added so much more diversity. Not only did he have perfect metronome timing, he hit really hard. He was able to go in between all the dynamics that we wanted to experiment with. It was just perfect. Plus he sang backup vocals and I'd wanted that ever since the beginning of the band." Once again, Cobain and Novoselic had gone about their business covertly. Peters had no idea he'd been so rapidly replaced. When he later found out, in a casual phone call from Kurt, he felt grossly humiliated. His entire career with Nirvana amounted to one track, 'Sliver', and one gig, the Motor Sports Arena.

A couple of months later, Kurt told Melody Maker writer Push: "It wasn't that we were unhappy with Dan's drumming. It was just that Dave has qualities that match our needs a little closer...."

Nirvana issued a handwritten press statement to announce their new drummer. The statement went on to describe the two songs on the single, 'Sliver' ("poppy") and 'Dive' ("riffy, spiffy!!!"). It ended "The politburu [sic] of Kurt, Krist & Dave say good bye."

From the outset, then, the previously impervious two-man power base expanded to include the drummer. Anton Brookes made this connection in a remark to Everett True: "They became a rock band when Dave joined. He unified with Kurt and Krist - because for a long time it had just been those two, all the line down from school. He was the final piece in the jigsaw. Not only was he a powerhouse, he gave Nirvana a different dimension."

Grohl made his debut with Nirvana in Olympia, at the North Shore Surf Club, on October 11, and he fitted in brilliantly. Craig Montgomery told Carrie Borzillo: "Everything really came together then."

From the outset it was clear that Dave was hugely talented. He had learnt all of the songs for the shows in the space of about three weeks, and he was holding the band together better than Channing had ever managed. His playing was loud, direct and uncompromising; at times he seemed almost out of control and he destroyed several drum kits over the course of his first tour with Nirvana. As the destruction of equipment was already a theme of the band, he seemed ideally suited as a member of Nirvana as they rampaged their way across Britain.

Dave Grohl was born on January 14, 1969, in Warren, Ohio. He spent his first three years in the town of Columbus, with father James, a newspaper employee, mother Virginia, a high school English teacher, and elder sister Lisa. In 1972, the family moved to Springfield, Virginia, on the outskirts of Washington, DC, where three years later, the parents separated, leaving Virginia to bring up the children. At seven or eight, Dave took up the trombone and at age ten he had a life-changing experience when he saw the AC/DC film Let There Be Rock. Never had he imagined that music could sound so powerful and emotional: it made him want to smash something to pieces. This would be his stepping stone to hardcore and punk. In the meantime, Grohl formed his first band, the HG Hancock Band. At the age of 12, he received a guitar with a built-in amp for Christmas, then the next summer, he fell in love with punk. Dave had mixed well when he joined Thomas Jefferson High, being elected Vice President of his class and seems the school authorities tolerated his penchant for playing Circle Jerks and Bad Brains during the morning assembly. Presumably, they were unaware of his growing pot habit.

At 15, Grohl played guitar in a punk band called Freak Baby. This was the first of many groups for Dave, who quit school at 16. He went on to play with Mission Impossible - a hardcore outfit in which he started out as the guitarist and ended up as the drummer - and then Dain Bramage. This band mixed the rhythmic energy of hardcore with a rock sound influenced by Led Zeppelin, Tom Verlaine, Hüsker Dü and REM. They released an album, I Scream Not Coming Down, for an LA indie label. Then there was Harlingtox A.D., who never made it out of the studio. They did, however, record an EP, Harlingtox Angel Divine, which finally saw the light of day in 1996. At the time of this project, Grohl was already in Scream, who played rock and hardcore and had been heroes of his for several years before he'd answered an ad and joined them at 17.

Moving to Washington to take his place in Nirvana, Grohl lived first with Krist and Shelli Novoselic in Tacoma for six weeks and then with Kurt Cobain in Olympia. The flat was apparently "a fucking pit", according to Grohl.

Ten days after the Olympia gig, Nirvana, with Grohl on board, arrived in the UK for a week-long tour. They were accompanied, as ever, by Craig Montgomery and a new tour manager, Alex MacLeod. Supporting were L7, the spirited female punk band from LA.

Everywhere they went in the UK, the vibe was unmistakeable, the understanding unanimous, the outcome inevitable: Nirvana was going to happen, massively. Kurt seemed to know it too. Sounds published the interview that Keith Cameron had conducted with the fleeting Dan Peters line-up of the band, and Cobain memorably stated that, "All my life my dream has to be a big rock star."

Melody Maker's Push, interviewing the band, described 'Sliver' - the single which should have been but wasn't released in the UK in time for the tour - as "a hell of a pop song". Finally issued in December, it was reviewed in Melody Maker by Everett True, who wrote: "Sure, the vocals are lazily throat splitting, the guitars belligerently grungy, the bass up and out of the place, but check the melodies, damn fools, check the melodies."

Everett had, unsurprisingly, figured in Nirvana's British appearances, appearing onstage as The Legend! at the last show in Nottingham. Introduced by Cobain, he got part-way through 'Do Nuts' (a song he'd recorded for Sub Pop) before Krist and Kurt, who had both been drumming, decided instead to trash the kit.

There was some resistance to Dave Grohl's appointment. While most observers applauded his tough drumming power, his aggression and his ability to draw everything together with immense energy, others preferred the less precise style of a Chad Channing. Dave, they felt, was too professional. There were also fans who believed that Grohl's drumming was too rocky, too simple, too punchy.

Back in Washington for the winter, Kurt Cobain was moping around after his October break-up with Tobi Vail. Although it had happened at his own instigation, he was truly miserable. He started scribbling poems that expressed his hurt and anger, self-critical sentiments that also lashed out at others. Some of these wounded cries found their way into the lyrics of Nevermind.

Despite Kurt's dire depression, it seems to be a coincidence that around this time he started using heroin regularly. Heroin use had been escalating in Seattle and Olympia since the beginning of the year, particularly in musicians' circles. Novoselic and Grohl were horrified. Cobain reassured them that he didn't like the drug anyway and would stay away from it in future. Instead, he and Dylan Carlson snuck off on their own to shoot up.

Nirvana made two live appearances locally before the end of the year. One, on November 25, was at Seattle's Off Ramp club, which organised a lock-in so the band could play on after time. It was there that Dan Peters finally understood his ousting in favour of Dave Grohl, telling Everett True: "It made perfect sense to me. I was like, 'He's the fucking guy for the job.'" The other show was on New Year's Eve at the Satyricon Club in Portland, Oregon, described by True as "another sold-out whirlwind of bruised limbs and braised emotion".

By the end of 1990, the band had become completely disillusioned with their record label. Sub Pop had very poor distribution and almost no money to put behind the projects they took on. To an idealistic punk band that had no other way of getting their music heard, this situation had been acceptable, and the label's support had been vital in gaining the band some local credibility. But now, with their rising popularity, it was clear Nirvana needed something more from their record label, in order to maintain their momentum. Simply having an end product was no longer good enough, and the fact that Sub Pop was having trouble supporting the likes of Mudhoney made it obvious the label couldn't afford to put any real money behind a new Nirvana record.

The band began seeking advice about its position with Sub Pop, having discussions with Ken Goes, the manager of The

Pixies, and Susan Silver, who also looked after Soundgarden. Although these early meetings came to nothing, it was a sign that Nirvana wanted to move; and when Kurt and Krist were invited to the MCA building in LA, it was clear that other companies were interested help them to do it.

The members of Nirvana however, were unimpressed with the way record companies treated them as a second-class act. The people at MCA were typical of this: although they put the band up in an expensive hotel and paid for everything they wanted during the two day trip, it was obvious that no-one within the company, save for the A&R man who had spotted them on their west coast tour, had actually listened to the band's music. Record companies were still looking for something like the big earners of the time, as the pop music made by Michael Jackson and rock music by Guns n' Roses was raking in big dollars. They saw no reason to tamper with the formula and pay any serious attention to music from bands like Nirvana, because they were, by definition, unmarketable, uncooperative and underground.

The band therefore decided to make a concerted effort to get management representation, in order to get the most out of the companies that were failing to give them the same respect as other artists. Although some record companies were convinced that grunge wouldn't catch on, Nirvana was still gaining a lot of interest. Even if they were second-class, it was clear they had an energy that struck a chord with a huge number of fans in the US and Europe.

Thurston Moore, of Sonic Youth, had recommended that Nirvana take on Gold Mountain as managers, the company responsible for representing Moore's band. And so the band signed with Gold Mountain, most probably because they were great admirers of Sonic Youth. Their new management didn't have to work too hard to impress them; simply representing one of the best bands around at the time was sufficient. So Nirvana was now properly represented, and they were ready to build on their prior successes.

The first step Gold Mountain took was to organise a gig to be attended by A&R people from all the record labels that might have been interested in Nirvana at the time. The performance took place on November 25, 1990, and there were more record company representatives in attendance than there were Nirvana fans. It was a great gig, with the set consisting almost entirely of new material; and the crowd, considering it was made up of mostly businessmen, went wild. Kurt regularly referred to it as his favourite Nirvana performance, and it was a sentiment that wasn't overlooked by the crowd of A&R people.

Over the course of a few hours after the gig, the band received a stack of offers from record companies, and initially favoured Charisma Records. It was, however, DGC that the band eventually settled on, and it was this company that would help build the band up to the stratospheric heights it would later reach.

DGC was a subsidiary of Geffen, and was the record label that put out Sonic Youth's music. This may have been a key factor in the decision; Nirvana loved the idea of being on the same label. Moreover, Gold Mountain knew the company and could vouch for them. Crucially, DGC would be able to ensure proper distribution of the group's records and as a part of Geffen - a huge company - DGC had access to a massive amount of working capital, should it be required. By joining DGC, Nirvana had made a conscious effort to leave behind all the problems that had so annoyed them during their time with Sub Pop. This decision would prove to be a wise one.

As a part of the deal, the band would receive an advance of $287,000 for their next record, a figure almost unheard of for a grunge band. But they would have to wait several months before they would get their hands on their the money. On the face of it nothing had changed, but in reality the band was setting in motion the events that would launch them to the top of almost every chart worldwide. By the time they were able spend their advance, they would be just months away from the release of Nevermind, and from becoming the most famous grunge band of all time.

In Seattle and Portland, the band's popularity was positively booming. Slim Moon told Carrie Borzillo: "In late '90, early '91, they got a lot bigger. I remember Dave Grohl saying something about being at the laundromat doing his laundry, and he was living in Olympia with Kurt, and some kids were like, 'Aren't you in Nirvana? What are you doing, doing your own laundry?'"

Their next recordings would validate every enthusiastic word that had been written about them. They began work on New Year's Day 1991 in Seattle's Music Source studios where they recorded and mixed seven songs. This version of 'Even In His Youth' emerged as the B-side on the 'Smells Like Teen Spirit' single, while 'Aneurysm' accompanied it on certain formats. These were the only two songs with finished vocals. Nirvana also crashed through 'On A Plain', 'All Apologies', 'Token Eastern Song' and two instrumentals: 'Oh, The Guilt' and 'Radio Friendly Unit Shifter'.

The session was historic for two reasons: it was Dave Grohl's studio debut with Nirvana, and it was the first time they'd been produced by their tour sound engineer Craig Montgomery. Montgomery later said: "They had been playing 'Aneurysm' live a lot, and it was really huge with the tom fills and the vocals coming in and the way the guitar goes from clean to dirty. What I was trying to get was the feel of a live show. Kurt's ability to scream like that was always otherworldly to me."

Also in January, Sub Pop released their last Nirvana record

- a split single featuring Nirvana's 'Molly's Lips', a Vaselines cover and live favourite that later featured on Incesticide, and The Fluid's 'Candy'. It came out as the 27th special from the Sub Pop Singles Club, and it was part of the buy-out deal between Geffen and Sub Pop - although Nirvana would not sign on DGC's dotted line until April. It was a fitting end to the relationship between the up-and-coming band and the independent record label. On the vinyl was pressed the word 'Later', a farewell from one to the other.

"Hello," said Kurt Cobain as Nirvana took the stage at Seattle's OK Hotel on April 17. "We're major-label corporate rock sell outs." This would become one of the most famous Nirvana gigs of all time, because it was here, at a packed venue being filmed for a documentary - Hype - about the Seattle sound, that they played 'Smells Like Teen Spirit' for the first time.

Jonathan Poneman told Everett True about his first hearing of this future rock classic: "When it started I remember thinking, 'Wow, this is a good song,' like, 'Wow, this is a really catchy verse'... and then it came to the chorus, and it was like time had stopped still for a second. Everyone was like, 'This has got to be one of the greatest choruses I've ever heard in my life.' The reaction was instantaneous. The crowd went absolutely crazy."

The song made an unforgettable impact on everyone who heard it that night. Former K musician Rich Jensen said it "just slayed". Nils Bernstein, president of the Nirvana fan club, told Carrie Borzillo: "I was standing there next to Kurt Bloch from the Fastbacks and we just looked at each other like, 'What was that?' I was totally riveted."

James Burdyshaw, formerly from a grunge outfit called Cat Butt, described what Nirvana sounded like to him at this time in a conversation with True: "When Nirvana were great, they were like beauty coming out of the darkness. They were a weird, nasty, dirty metal band, but they were also a sweet pop band."

This version of 'Smells Like Teen Spirit' was later released on With The Lights Out.

Cobain's "corporate rock sell outs" introduction to the audience may have been intended to disarm any hostility with self-deprecation and humour, but it referred to an uncomfortable truth. While Nirvana wanted major-label backing and planned to exist with integrity in that set-up, they knew they would be confronted with a certain amount of antipathy in Seattle and Olympia where musicians wore their badge of independence with pride. Dave Grohl told Spin magazine: "And now we're snubbed by people who think we're big rock stars." It was a situation that Kurt Cobain never really resolved in his own mind, despite his declaration to Sounds' Keith Cameron that he'd always wanted to be a "big rock star". Realising the dream would bring a dark cloud of guilt and self-disgust.

Vig later said: "I knew 'Smells Like Teen Spirit' was going to be one of the key tracks on the record. It was just amazingly powerful."

'Teen Spirit' - Kurt's effort to write "the ultimate pop song" after the example of Pixies - leaped out at everybody who heard the tapes. Danny Goldberg recalled: "All of us when we heard the rough mixes knew it was an incredible song."

Armed with these new tracks and a relatively new drummer, the band headed to California to start the real work on the record. They stayed in an apartment together and made daily trips to Sound City Studios, where they and Vig would work on the tracks. The sessions were slightly hampered by the fact that the band had barely finished writing the music for the record, and they spent hours agonising over slight changes. The lyrics were rarely finished very long before the final few takes, and so it was hard to get through things with the speed they had done in the past. The band soon become frustrated by the difficulties they encountered. Whereas in the past they had managed to get nine songs down in the space of six hours, with an end product they were happy with, now they were taking three weeks to record 10 songs.

The anger may have been beneficial for the sound they were aiming for, but it was making the process of recording harder. During one failed take for 'Lithium', Kurt was unhappy with his guitar part and smashed his guitar repeatedly on the floor, until it was in pieces all over the studio. This take was actually used in the final production of the record, when Vig added it on the end of 'Something in the Way' as a bonus track, entitled 'Endless, Nameless'.

The additional, happy, result of the time the band took over the sessions was that the album ended up sounding exactly as they had intended and it was certainly more coherent than Bleach. The tracks had all been finalised and recorded in the same six-week period, and the unity of mood was noticeable in the recordings. This was a complete album, rather than a collection of demos strung together to make a full length record. The recording was finished by late May, and in June they began to master the record and design the artwork that was to accompany it. Kurt had always been an aspiring artist, and so it was his intention to design the sleeve art for the album, which was initially to be called Sheep but by this stage had taken on the name it would eventually be released under. Inspired by a documentary he had seen on water birth, Kurt decided on the picture of a newborn child swimming underwater chasing after a dollar bill. The back of the album was to feature a collage of Kurt's sculptures of meat and female genitalia, along with a toy monkey he had had for years.

The final mix of the album wasn't exactly what DGC wanted, and so they approached the band and asked for some changes in the production. The band were happy with the way Vig had produced the album, but as the record was already over budget — the original $65,000 they had set aside for the sessions had blown out to $120,000 over the six-week period — the band decided to listen to their record company. Arguing that the record would appeal to a wider audience when played on the radio if it was remixed by another producer, DGC managed to bring the band round. Andy Wallace, who was one of the most versatile producers of the time, having worked on the Run-DMC collaboration with Aerosmith on the single 'Walk This Way', as well as producing tracks for Slayer, Bruce Springsteen and Prince, was brought in to remix the album and to add a more 'instant' sound to the record.

Nirvana were concerned that Wallace had toned down some of their tumultuous punk fury, had sugared the pill somewhat, but this was exactly what made Nevermind such a worldwide sensation.

Cobain explained, ""You don't know what it's going to really sound like until you take it home and it's on a tape and you listen to it over and over again. At that point, after we attempted to mix Nevermind for like two weeks, we were so burnt out on it that we just didn't even care anymore. By the time we got Andy Wallace in, it was just like 'Oh, yeah, this is fine!'" However, it was clear that Wallace - if no one else - had his eyes on the prize, as he had managed to alleviate the band's pop-rock leanings, and in the process had created a mainstream pop-rock sound that others still attempt to duplicate to this day.

The record had enormous power but its gigantic crossover appeal came from its colour, its melody and dynamics, the use of contrast making Kurt's anguished wailing and the band's murderous outbursts all the more hair-raisingly dramatic.

At this point the record was still in the final stages of merchandising, and wouldn't be put out for some months, but the band were touring, playing the new material and building the hype around its upcoming release. 'Smells Like Teen Spirit' was marking itself out as the hit, and within DGC there was a buzz that the record would be bigger than expected. Original expectations were that the album would shift around 50,000 copies, but after a show put on especially for the DGC and Geffen executives, the band worked hard enough to impress the label, raising their estimate to 100,000. They were doing the impossible: getting respect from record company executives and starting to be treated as a first-class concern. Nirvana would soon discover, too, that they had become radio- and TV- friendly.

This was all bad, according to the hard-line musicians' mafia in Washington. Nirvana had lost their soul, sniped Chad Channing. They'd betrayed their individuality, huffed Charles Peterson. Eventually, Nirvana would be blamed for the hordes of fame-seeking bands and individuals who flocked to Seattle to try to catch some of its stardust, trampling all over the purity of what had been happening in the first place.

One of these characters was Courtney Love, a loud, outrageous and phenomenally ambitious chaser of rock dreams.

She travelled from Portland, Oregon, to Seattle, but whatever she was looking for, she didn't find it in the rainy city. She stuck it out for a couple of days before heading south to LA. And it was there, at the Palladium in May 1991 - at a gig featuring the Butthole Surfers, Red Kross and L7 - that she met Kurt.

Everett True had just befriended Courtney. He was crazy about the wildness of the woman and her music. When Cobain walked into the VIP area to see Everett and Courtney fighting drunkenly on the floor, he did what came naturally: he joined in, and was "formally" introduced to his future wife by True.

In June, Nirvana toured the West Coast opening for Dinosaur Jr, where they introduced some more of the Nevermind material into their set. 'Drain You made its first appearance in San Francisco on June 13, and 'Endless, Nameless' also received an airing on this tour as did the unsettling 'Rape Me' - a song that would be released much later, on In Utero.

According to many who saw the shows, Nirvana stole all the glory from the headliners. Danny Goldberg - who'd signed the band to Gold Mountain on the recommendations of John Silva and Thurston Moore - suddenly realised their genius at the Hollywood Palladium on June 14. He told Carrie Borzillo that it was an "epiphany", adding: "The bond between Kurt and the audience was so amazing. I knew I was witnessing history. There was an intimacy he had with this audience that I had just never seen in my life before."

The atmosphere around the band at this time was like waiting for a bomb to go off: everyone felt it. Kurt Cobain later told Rolling Stone that, "There was so much excitement in the air you could taste it."

The crowds were getting bigger and more fanatical. The journalists who had always supported Nirvana were on tenterhooks, waiting for the inevitable explosion. The Geffen/DGC and Gold Mountain staff that attended a packed showcase at LA's small Roxy club on August 15 came away swearing they'd be telling their grandchildren about this one. The radio DJs who were starting to receive copies of 'Smells Like Teen Spirit' were simply gobsmacked. Kurt St Thomas, musical director of Boston's alternative station WFNX, was the first recipient. He put it on heavy rotation straight away, predicting it would change the face of music. Listeners bombarded the station with requests. Record stores were submitting unheard of large orders for an untested band.

And so it was with this gathering expectation of greatness surrounding them that Nirvana set off on a European tour with Sonic Youth on August 19, both bands being filmed alongside others they played with along the way - Mudhoney, Dinosaur Jr, Ramones, Gumball and Black Francis - for a video film titled 1991: The Year Punk Broke. The documentary shows Cobain at his most excited about his music, and the level of success that the band were achieving.

"It was incredible," he said. "I mean, to be asked to go on tour by a band like Sonic Youth was like a dream come true. I still can't describe what I felt. It was like, wow, what an honour. It was great and the momentum and excitement at the time was so great, because everyone sensed that the album was going to do pretty well. There was just a feeling in the air; there was just like this new thing happening. No one could quite pinpoint it, but we knew that we were a part of it," he added.

He was also quick to credit the influence that the Manhattan scenesters had upon Nirvana at the time, detailing his feelings in an interview in 1992. However his words already betrayed some weariness and cynicism: "We just basically do everything that Sonic Youth does. We just steal all their ideas. That's what we're turning into now. If you saw the show tonight, if you saw that last thing we did, whatever you wanna call it, we're turning into a noise guitar prog rock band. Hey, that's the next step for any band! But they've been doing it for years before anyone else. Honestly, I feel kind of burnt out with the formula that we've been doing. We've been in this band for like six years and playing pop music can get a bit redundant, so I think we all wanna start experimenting, and really the only alternative you have is to turn into Sonic Youth."

"One of the first shows we played with them was at the Reading Festival. There had been alternative bands playing the Reading Festival for the last three or four years. We didn't know anything about it. We never knew that that thing existed. To walk out onstage in front of that many people, and to realise that that many people like this kind of music, it was just like, 'Wow, where have we been? Under a rock all these years?' But then again, Europe is a bit different than America, too. I mean, America's quite a few years behind."

Reading was at that time the most prestigious event on the UK's festival calendar, and Nirvana were modestly placed on a bill headlined by Iggy Pop and Sonic Youth, onstage in the afternoon. A daylight show was not ideal, and the wind blew the sound all over the place, but Nirvana triumphed spectacularly. They were "stunning, ferocious, on fire", said Everett True. The audience sang along, word perfect, with 'Smells Like Teen Spirit', even though it hadn't been released: Nirvana bootlegs were clearly in huge demand. At the end of the set, they beat up their gear, with Kurt reportedly dislocating his shoulder as he flung himself in his usual reckless manner into the drum kit.

Whatever the extent of his injury, Nirvana were back onstage the next day, at another festival in Koln, Germany, and they carried on through the tour, devastating audiences, drinking heavily, having food fights and setting off fire extinguishers.

Mudhoney also played at the festival; and although they were still considered to be bigger than their fellow Northwest outfit, in terms of performance, Nirvana was staking its claim on the grunge crown. The scale of the tour differed to that of the band's previous European tour. Rather than playing a lot of gigs to capacity crowds in small venues, the band now found themselves playing only 10 dates, several of which were festivals, performing in front of up to 70,000 people. This was a massive step up to the big time for the band, and they seemed well suited to it.

In August 1991, Nirvana was gearing up for a level of fame and popularity nobody could have imagined possible, and they were doing it where they had their largest fan base: in Europe. Whilst in the UK they paid a visit to one of their greatest supporters in the country at the time, John Peel, recording a session for his radio show before heading back to Olympia. This was a nod to the dedicated patronage the legendary broadcaster had given them.

Things were a little different in Olympia when Kurt returned from the European tour, and not just because Dave Grohl had recently moved from the sofa in their appalling shared flat to a rented house in Seattle. It was more that the alternative community in Olympia, the city that had shaped and encouraged Kurt's musical and personal philosophies, was now rejecting him because of his growing success. For Cobain to be cut off so decisively by the people he most admired was for him the cruellest aspect of Nirvana's rise to fame.

In Europe, and particularly England, journalists were lining up to talk to Nirvana - a direct result of their incendiary Reading Festival appearance. They were entering the mainstream. Cobain distrusted the press, and he disliked inane questions and musical ignorance as much as he abhorred the idea of himself as a rock icon. He soon started refusing to give radio interviews, much to the horror of Geffen. None of the band felt any responsibility to modify their normal behaviour simply because they were on a major label. Hence they got chucked out of their own album launch party at Seattle's Re-Bar on September 13 after yet another food fight.

'Smells Like Teen Spirit' had been released days earlier. The album - which had already been previewed in its entirety by WFNX's Kurt St Thomas - followed on September 24. In a press release announcing its release, Kurt was quoted as saying, "Punk is musical freedom. It's saying, doing and playing what you want. The word nirvana means freedom from pain, suffering and the external world, and that's pretty close to my definition of punk rock."

By now, the band had started their Nevermind tour of the States and Canada. 'Teen Spirit' had been picked up by MTV. One downside was that Geffen had underestimated the massive demand for the record, which was flying out of the shops as fast as it could be delivered. No one had expected the massive demand for Nirvana.

At the time, Grohl expressed his disbelief at the band's new-found fame, saying that when they "came home it was like the Beatles. It was like Nirvana mania stepping off the plane; there weren't a bunch of kids waiting with banners but ...," he laughed as Cobain added "It was just the right album at the right time. I mean, I'm sure there was a collective consciousness. People were tired of everything else - it just got old. Just like grunge music will be in a couple of years, if it hasn't already. If we don't progress, if we don't change, if we don't take chances and do different things."

Unsurprisingly, Everett True reviewed the single for Melody Maker. He whooped: "Single of the year, in case you were wondering how to fill in those Readers' Polls." Simon Reynolds, writing in the New York Times, commented: "'Smells Like Teen Spirit' could be this generation's version of the Sex Pistols' 1976 single, 'Anarchy In The UK', if it weren't for the bitter irony that pervades its title. As Nirvana knows only too well, teen spirit is routinely bottled, shrink-wrapped and sold. Mr Cobain, acutely aware of the contradiction of operating in an industry that's glad to turn rebellion into money, rails against the passivity of today's youth. The song's defiance quickly disintegrates into despondency and fatalism. The song is an anthem for kids who don't know what they want, and probably wouldn't have the willpower to get it even if they did."

Kurt, however, maintained it was a more personal piece of writing, telling Hits magazine journalist Roy Trakin that it was "mainly just me dealing with my own apathy rather than attacking my generation and accusing them of being apathetic".

The single had been intended to draw in audiences from a range of different tastes, and hopefully get played on a number of different radio stations, rather than just the rock shows. This plan, however, backfired.

For starters, a great number of US stations refused to play it, claiming on-air that it was too aggressive for their pop shows;

none of the crossover occurred, simply because the DJs couldn't see the poppiness that was in the songwriting. The power of grunge came from the underground demand: the music was already out there in the public domain and all it took was for kids to phone in and request the track for it to get air-time. The fact was that, although the DJs thought it inappropriate - perhaps because the DJs thought it inappropriate - people wanted to hear it. By denying their listeners the track, they had actually encouraged people to listen to it. This only served to exemplify the power of music that had been made by a disengaged section of the community. Grunge music had found its audience.

Without intending it, DGC had put out a hit single and created a whirlwind of hype based on the unprecedented success of this debut single. Almost every mainstream radio station was now playing 'Smells Like Teen Spirit', and so the American public was preparing itself for the rest of the record. When it arrived they found that it was filled with a similar sounding collection of tracks; similar in mood and tone, and similar in the fact that they sounded like nothing else on their favourite radio stations. There was certainly a cleaner sound to the record when compared to Bleach, and to the other albums from the grunge movement up until its release, but the majority of radio listeners weren't listening to Mudhoney, and Nevermind was certainly no cleaner sound than any other mainstream record at the time.

Songs such as 'Territorial Pissings' and 'In Bloom' were not like typical tracks found on a number one record in the US, especially in 1991, when the top selling album of the year was Mariah Carey's self-titled debut. On first listen the songs can sound like disorganised jams, with a maniac screaming over the top of them; but they were hitting the right notes with the record buying public. This was a revolution, in musical terms, and it heralded the start of a wave of rock acts breaking into the mainstream as Nirvana began to be played on MTV. The music channel was to be a big supporter of Nirvana, and the regular airings of 'Smells Like Teen Spirit' from November 1991 onwards helped spread the band's music even further. It was clear that everything they did was going to elicit a huge response from the public.

Nirvana were touring the States as the single and album were beginning their long but steady climb up the charts. With 'Teen Spirit' on heavy rotation on MTV, the audiences were not only much bigger but were filling up with a cross-section of people, not just the usual grungy types. Everywhere, fans and critics commented on Dave Grohl, and how much strength he'd brought to the band. Greg Kot of the Chicago Tribune stated that Dave "transformed the band into this incredible powerhouse". The Seattle Times reported that the songs were "tighter... more condensed and delivered with a new sense of confidence and style. A good deal of credit has to go to Dave Grohl..." These remarks were typical in the reviews Nirvana was now receiving.

Arriving in Chicago on October 12, Kurt received a visitor in his dressing room. Courtney Love had just split up with Smashing Pumpkins' Billy Corgan - now she had her sights set on Cobain, who had been enjoying a romance with Boston indie singer Mary Lou Lord. Typically trying to avoid a confrontation, Kurt juggled his relationships with both women for a month until the tour reached England - where Mary Lou was shocked to discover she'd been ousted in favour of Courtney.

Not only were the crowds larger and more diverse, they were also wilder. In Dallas on October 19, Kurt was famously beaten up onstage when he tried to stop one of the security men manhandling the fans. There were riotous scenes in Tijuana, Mexico, reported by John Godfrey in the San Diego Union-Tribune: "A sold-out crowd explored the limits of sanity (and safety) in what was the most violent pop show this critic has ever witnessed. Crazed music fans leaped from 18-foot balconies on to other, similarly crazed music fans below, countless people fell in the slam pits and were trampled by fellow-moshers; the security guards didn't even try to prevent more than a hundred people from diving headlong off the stage."

The crowds were huge, or at least they were huge compared to the venues. The tour had been booked before the record was released, and was another sign of how DGC had underestimated the band's potential popularity. The shows took place in medium-sized venues across the country, and they simply weren't big enough. In several places the gigs had been oversold, and patrons were crammed in, far exceeding the capacity of the venues; they would climb pillars and spill onto the stage area, all of which was a huge distraction for the musicians, who were simply trying to play a set.

The conditions they were playing under started to grate with the band, and, as was traditional on a Nirvana tour, tensions were high. At one event, after diving into the audience with his guitar, Kurt was grabbed by a bouncer, and proceeded to smash the offending assistant in the head with his instrument. A small fight ensued, and Kurt ran for cover in the venue. The bouncer was taken to a hospital, and it wasn't until he was off the premises that the front man came out from his hiding place.

In LA, rock luminaries such as Motley Crüe drummer Tommy Lee and Axl Rose turned out to see Nirvana (much to Kurt's displeasure) at a show benefiting the Rock For Choice abortion rights organisation, set up by L7 to support the Feminist Majority Foundation. That same night, Kurt - resplendent in a yellow dress - filmed an interview with Novoselic for MTV's Headbanger's Ball. From now on it would not be unusual to see him in women's clothing - or with multi-coloured hair. He had recently dyed it blue to enliven the many photo sessions Nirvana now had to endure.

Halloween night, October 31, marked a heroes' return - and a goodbye - to the Seattle clubs where they had learned their trade. There was no doubt now that Nirvana was destined for rock stardom. Nevermind was scaling the Billboard chart in leaps and bounds and it had just gone gold when they appeared at the Paramount, supported by Bikini Kill and Mudhoney, in front of an audience teeming with journalists and record label and management figures. Scenes filmed at the gig were later used in the video for 'Lithium', and this performance of 'Negative Creep' was released on the live album, From The Muddy Banks Of The Wishkah. This was when Kurt's deep unease with his growing celebrity started really to kick in. Amid all the party celebrations backstage at the Paramount, witnesses remember him looking disturbed and withdrawn, erecting an invisible barrier between himself and the gangs of hangers-on.

The tour was a huge success, in terms of revenue and promotion. By the time the band got back to Seattle, at the end of October, Nevermind had gone gold, selling over 500,000 copies. But in terms of the band dynamic, it had been ropey. One of the key reasons was Kurt's increasing use of drugs. None of the band had stayed clean from anything for a long time, and Krist and Kurt had a long history of experimenting with all sorts of mind-expanding substances; but the difference was what drug Kurt was using. He had started to inject heroin, which was something the other two roundly disapproved of. Heroin was putting distance between Kurt, who was the main songwriter, and Krist and Dave. It had been most evident on the latest tour, where the band was continuing to play the kind of gigs they had played prior to Nevermind, but were beginning to be idolised. Kurt was spending his time away from the others, high, and this left Krist and Dave with a sense that they had been rejected in favour of heroin, Kurt's new best friend.

Nirvana fever soared in America but the band was not there

to see it. They were touring Europe. The six-week trek opened on November 4 with the first of two batches of English dates. This included a performance on the TV show, The Word, where Kurt announced to Britain - and a shaken Mary Lou Lord - that, "Courtney Love, of the pop group Hole, is the best fuck in the world!"

Nirvana received reams of prestigious press coverage. The November issue of Rolling Stone contained a review of Nevermind by the highly regarded critic Ira Robbins. Hedging his bets, Robbins marked the album at three out of five, stating that, "the thrashing Nevermind boasts an adrenalized pop heart and incomparably superior material [to that on Bleach], captured with roaring clarity by co-producer Butch Vig". Praising Nirvana's "skill at inscribing subtlety on to dense, noisy rock", Robbins concluded: "Nevermind finds Nirvana at the crossroads - scrappy garageland warriors setting their sights on a land of giants."

Simon Reynolds - a British journalist writing for publications on both sides of the Atlantic - addressed the lyrical aspects of the album in the New York Times: "In speaking to the press, Nirvana's singer-guitarist, Kurt Cobain, comes across as anti-jingo-ist, anti-redneck, anti-misogynist, anti-materialist and so on. But on Nevermind, Nirvana's rage is mostly unspecific and apolitical, and at times verges on incoherent. It provides a catch-all catharsis that fits in perfectly with the directionless disaffection of the 20-something generation."

Reynolds was also writing about Nirvana for English newspapers. In the issue of The Observer dated December 8 - the week that 'Smells Like Teen Spirit' hit its highest position of Number Seven in the UK (it would peak at one place higher in the Billboard chart) - he sounded a warning, with justification: "Nirvana is aware that there's a danger that some fans won't notice the subtitles but merely get off on the surface violence. It's the perennial dilemma of crossover; whether it's better to lurk safely in the womb-like security of indie cult-hood or make a change and risk being misunderstood or corrupted."

In Melody Maker the same month, Reynolds reviewed the band's London Kilburn National show, which largely disappointed him, but he noted: "When they do shake off the sluggishness, stop goofing around, and hit their stride, Nirvana are magnificent. By the last encore, you feel Nirvana are finally unleashed, raging full on. . ." Concluding, he caught an undeniable truth: "At the moment, they're uncomfortably poised between their Sub Pop slob-rock past and their future rock godhood. They seem embarrassed and bemused, it's like their boots are too big for them."

Ben Thompson, reviewing the Kilburn gig for the Independent On Sunday, similarly noticed their "rejection of traditional rock star profligacy", quoting a line from the Slacker movie to support their stance: "Withdrawing in disgust is not apathy." Unlike Reynolds, Thompson found Nirvana and their "animal ferocity" gripping from the outset. Likening them to "a band trapped inside a video game", he decided that this was no bad thing, no passive surrender. Instead, he said, "Nirvana's name is as much an ironic shot at middle American mindlessness as a statement of belief in the considerable redemptive power of what they do. They are a reaction - and a magnificently psychotic one at that - to the passivity of a rock culture whose only function is to be consumed."

Taking up the point of "traditional rock star profligacy", Rich Jensen summed up one particular aspect of Kurt's dilemma in The True Story: "He encapsulates the problem of being a band of men engaging in this traditional macho practice while having sympathies that run completely counter to that practice. I think Kurt understood that complication completely. It's one of the things that makes it worth talking about even today."

Other people who knew Kurt, including True, observed that

he also worried about the consequences of A-list touring. Cobain appreciated his audiences, he enjoyed the validation that came with Nirvana's burgeoning success, but it also compromised their credibility and core values of spontaneity, intimacy and fun. They were corporate property now, and despite their frequent bids to buck the system, they had to play the game. There was pressure all the time, little privacy, little rest and little escape from the monster they'd created.

"We resented the success so we turned into assholes," said Kurt to Michael Azerrad. "We got drunk a lot and wrecked more equipment than we needed to. We just decided to be real abusive pricks. We wanted to make life miserable for people."

Meanwhile, NME had had to stop sulking about the fact that its competitor, Melody Maker, courtesy of Everett True, had introduced Nirvana to the British public. It sent writer Edwin Pouncey to Italy for a major feature on the band. He wrote of the "pure, unfettered excitement" of the gig in Muggia, and of Krist Novoselic's optimism that they could cope with constant touring. At the same time, Pouncey depicted Cobain as an isolated figure who admitted that "There are times when we don't wanna do encores because we're not having enough fun…"

The second bunch of UK dates - with Nirvana supported by the Japanese all-girl garage-pop outfit Shonen Knife - was followed by a one-off in France and the sudden cancellation of the remaining tour dates in Ireland and Scandinavia. Kurt had been suffering from chronic stomach pain and his attempts to treat it with cough mixture and booze had not helped greatly. Nirvana were also said to be stressed and suffering from the cumulative effects of too much alcohol. They returned to the States to find Nevermind in the Billboard Top Five and they ended the year in front of manic crowds in a string of shows on a triple bill with Pearl Jam and Red Hot Chili Peppers.

CHAPTER 6

Nevermind finally made it to Number One in Billboard in the second week of January 1992, five months after its initial release, having sold two million copies, with an almost bewildered DGC president Ed Rosenblatt remarking: "We didn't do anything. It was just one of those 'get out of the way and duck' records." In fact, the only reason that Nevermind had not climbed straight to the top of the charts was the failure of the record company to press enough copies. However, it was a triumph tinged with darkness.

On January 10, the LA music paper Bam was the first to print a story linking Kurt Cobain with heroin. Writer Jerry McCulley had interviewed him backstage at the 16,000-capacity Sports Arena during the Pearl Jam/Chili Peppers series, reporting that Kurt was "nodding off occasionally in mid-sentence. He's had but an hour's sleep, he says blearily. But the pinned pupils; sunken cheeks; and scabbed, sallow skin suggest something more serious than mere fatigue."

Both Kurt and Geffen reacted furiously, Cobain raging at McCulley and Bam - "one of the shittiest, cock-rock-oriented LA magazines" - for getting it so wrong. This must have been galling for McCulley who, in fact, had hit upon the truth. Later, Kurt confessed that he had been taking smack during the recent European tour. Krist Novoselic and Dave Grohl admitted they'd had no idea how to approach Cobain about what was clearly happening as they travelled Europe, particularly since Kurt was now, as he said himself, "blinded by love" for his latest flame. Withdrawing from his bandmates - since heroin powerfully bonds users, to the exclusion of almost anyone else - he closeted himself away with Courtney. To the consternation of everyone around them, they pursued their love affair with each other and with smack.

On January 11, alarm bells really started ringing about Kurt's condition. He missed a daytime photo session and spent more than an hour trying (or not trying) to get out of his hotel for a prestigious appearance on NBC's Saturday Night Live. He was sick on the way to the studio. Once there, he spent an hour in the bathroom with Courtney and passed out in the dressing room before filming began. He was "so fucked up", according to his press officer Lisa Gladfelter Bell.

Danny Goldberg told Carrie Borzillo: "Somewhere around Saturday Night Live is when it started to become clear that there was a drug problem. Between that time and the time he died, it was a constant series of discussions and meetings and ups and downs with a series of different people."

Craig Montgomery also cites this show as the moment when everyone around Nirvana realised Kurt had a major problem. But the bandwagon rolled on at a dizzying rate with TV shows and video shoots and interviews for the front covers of magazines and music papers all over the world, not to mention the tours. Before the end of January, Nirvana were in the Antipodes, playing some dates and cancelling others, again because of Kurt's abdominal problems. He was, it's said, detoxing from heroin, but it would be a brief withdrawal. Australian journalist Murray Engleheart said that, "Due to his stomach agonies, Kurt, for the most part even at this point, kept to himself, thus unwittingly creating and accentuating his own mystique." But Nirvana could still pull it out of the bag. Engleheart wrote of their appearance at the first Big Day Out festival in Sydney: "There was an amazing sense of community, but for some the manic attraction also made for an event that ranked as one of their most frightening gig experiences. The fine line between fun and pure unbridled fear came close to being breached on many occasions."

They travelled on to New Zealand, Singapore and Japan, returning to the US where a smacked-out Kurt and a pregnant Courtney were married in Hawaii on February 24. That previously close friends such as the Novoselics and Craig Montgomery were not present attested to the divisions already forming within Nirvana, due to the happy couple's increasing drug use. From now on, although they were now among the world's most adored and sensational acts, the Kurt and Courtney sideshow was an inextricable part of the public perception of the band.

Promotional activities continued apace. Cobain appeared on MTV's Headbanger's Ball in drag, mocked the BBC's Top of the Pops tradition of having artists lip-synch on the show and their now regular destruction of instruments was immortalised in a performance on Saturday Night Live that ended with Novoselic and Grohl sharing a kiss. The Top Of The Pops performance featured changed lyrics - "load up on drugs and kill your friends" – which saw Cobain singing in an operatic baritone and Novoselic swinging his bass around his head like a lunatic. It certainly made an impact among the pop audience in Britain, as Nirvana became the talk of the playgrounds.

Similarly, the finale of the band's two-song performance on Saturday Night Live was their message to people at home—a signal that they couldn't be controlled by being put on television. At the end of 'Territorial Pissings', a song the show's producers had requested the band not play, they performed their traditional act of trashing their instruments. This was an act that had been proven to have great power when done live, but for an audience that was used to seeing cosy, well-produced TV, especially at the mid-evening timeslot that the program occupied, it was extraordinary. The members of the band were regular viewers of the program when they were growing up, and so this was their way of showing kids like them that they could upset the system they were a part of. Adding chaos to the evening TV schedule was an invitation to the youth of America to acknowledge the power and potential that they possessed.

As well as taking a stand against the media, the band soon turned their anger on their peers and a number of feuds began to arise, including the baiting of Pearl Jam's Eddie Vedder. Most noteworthy, however, was the band's ongoing rivalry with Guns N' Roses, and with their frontman Axl Rose in particular. Cobain pronounced with glee, "There is a war going on in the high schools now between Nirvana kids and Guns N' Roses kids. It's really cool. I'm really proud to be a part of that," adding, "I used to think that everything in the mainstream pop world was crap, but now that some underground bands have been signed with majors, I take Guns N' Roses as more of an offence. I have to look into it more. They're really talentless people, and they write crap music, and they're the most popular rock band on the earth right now. I can't believe it."

Seemingly, however, Kurt was also dissatisfied at his role in the band, and he began to distance himself form the others once more. One of the few communications they did have with each other was conducted through their lawyers, because Kurt wanted to change the royalty payments the band was receiving. At that point they were all receiving an equal share of the royalties, but because he was writing the music, Kurt believed he should get 75 per cent of the song writing credit and 100 per cent of the lyric royalties. This meant that the other band members' earnings would be dramatically cut; and because Kurt wanted the new agreement to cover all their previous recordings, it meant the other members of the band would actually owe him money. Krist and Dave were understandably upset. Kurt threatened to break up the band if they failed to comply, so there was little they could do; and as Nirvana had more tour dates fast approaching, the band members had to sweep their problems under the rug prior to embarking on another tour of Europe.

In the UK in February, Nevermind peaked at Number Seven, and 'Come As You Are' was released as a single. It reached Number Nine the next month; in the Billboard charts it stalled just outside the Top 30. By now, the grunge look - which was practical, affordable and unequivocally anti-style in its thrift-shop jumble of plaid shirts and torn jeans - had been appropriated by the fashion industry as the new chic. The Boston Globe told its readers that to achieve it, they should aim to look like a cross between a tramp and a prisoner of war.

Lisa Gladfelter Bell told Carrie Borzillo: "That was nauseating. The kind of magazines that never call you, like Vogue, were calling... Nirvana didn't try to start a fashion trend, it just happened."

Nirvana-mania was erupting across the United States while Nevermind was scooping all kinds of awards and sending A&R scouts into frenzied searches for "the next Nirvana". The band had returned to the US as heroes, and their days of touring small venues were officially over. They were now playing at celebrity-filled parties and massive arenas, and were spending their time hanging out with famous people, chatting to the bands that had inspired them to play music in the first place. Or at the very least they were trying to avoid being hassled by people who simply wanted to be friends with the biggest band of the moment. It was a sudden shift for the band, and they were finding it hard to comprehend. As a result, Kurt decided to come off the road and go into seclusion with Courtney in an LA flat where he spent months shooting up heroin and writing some of the material for In Utero.

Kurt's drug use was again placed under the spotlight in May, when Steve Hochman of the Los Angeles Times remarked that Nirvana's "low profile has renewed published speculation that singer/guitarist Kurt Cobain has a heroin problem". The official response cited Kurt's well-documented stomach ailment.

The rumours gathered pace when Nirvana regrouped in June to honour the shows they'd cancelled in Europe and Scandinavia at the end of 1991. The day after a concert in Belfast (during which Kurt once again came to blows with a security guard he saw laying into a fan), he was dramatically rushed to hospital. It was later explained that he was treated for a weeping ulcer which he'd had for some time due to a bad junk-food diet. This explanation was greeted with some scepticism when published in Melody Maker. Kurt later told Michael Azerrad that he was actually suffering from methadone withdrawal, having forgotten to take his tablets. Keith Cameron, interviewing the band for Sounds in July in Valencia, Spain, was explicit about Cobain's drug problems - he found the singer paranoid and uncommunicative - and about the divisions in the band. He suggested that Nirvana had gone from "nobodies to superstars to fuck-ups in the space of six months" and shook his head: "It was all doom and gloom."

When the band were on form, it was like old times. But, apparently, that didn't happen too often during the Irish and European dates. There were some positive reports. The Irish Times' Kevin Courtney said of the opening Dublin show: "Kurt Cobain's voice began ragged and rough as he screamed out the words of 'Drain You' and 'Stay Away'. But by the time the band launched into 'Lounge Act', he had harnessed the anger and venom that fuels his vocal power." Page Hamilton of Helmet, who appeared with Nirvana at the Roskilde Festival, said, "they were amazing. Those guys were so together, they had 60,000 Danish people singing along. It was fucking awesome."

Behind the scenes, Craig Montgomery described the atmosphere around the band as "pretty tense, and pretty professional". In addition to their internal difficulties, Nirvana, and Kurt in particular, were unhappy because they had now quite clearly become that dreaded thing - an arena act, which to them was worse than festivals. Cobain moaned to Everett True that he hated "kids with Bryan Adams and Bruce Springsteen T-shirts coming up to me and asking for autographs". Metal fans were regarded with equal disdain. Kurt felt that such apparently enthusiastic people were simply behaving ritually, treating Nirvana like every other act on the festival conveyor belt, missing the point of the music.

True posed another pertinent question: "How can anyone be rebellious once they've conquered the American market?" He also quoted Kurt as saying this: "I'm so far beyond thinking about the band that I can't let it bother me any more. It's so exhausting. I feel so raped that I have to just have fun now." The irony was that he didn't seem to be having any fun at all.

Everett had flown out to cover Nirvana in Stockholm and Oslo in July 1992 for Melody Maker, and he told its readers: "The world's only credible arena rock band is close to cracking. Kurt Cobain is barely able to cope with the restraints of his position. His band is afraid to play any new songs, knowing that - if they do - bootlegs will hit the streets running. So numbed by the intensity of their unlooked-for role as some kind of spokesmen, Nirvana attempt to inject meaning into the old the best they can, which means no emotion shown, if that's the only way they can retain self-respect."

In Oslo, at the Isle of Calf Festival, "Kurt simply stands immobile as 20,000 kids go berserk, uncaring as to what reactions his band may or may not be exciting." The band still sounded "glorious" and "life-affirming". Yet, True decided that the gig was "a mess of contradictions and contrary emotions". He realised that Kurt was "torn between his loyalty to the kids who genuinely appreciate and love his music, and those who are into them as a fad, as a cuter, punkier Ugly Kid Joe alternative.

His voice is still inexhaustibly expressive, emotive, his guitar still bleeds angst, but his demeanour... remember, this is the band who built a career out of being rampant on stage, whose new video mythologises the whole guitar-smashing ethos with a grandiose finality. Kurt won't even admit that he has any frustrations left. Not in public. But he has. Oh man."

Stockholm was a slightly better experience, since it was a dedicated Nirvana show and not a festival. But "the main set is still as bad as I've seen Nirvana play, in terms of spirit, excitement, inspiration (everything that Nirvana used to have in spades). Even if I am damn near crying during 'Lithium'..."

After two shows in Spain, Nirvana once again called off their final tour dates, this time because of a scare with Courtney's pregnancy. However, the seven-pound Frances Bean Cobain was born safe and well in LA's exclusive Cedars-Sinai hospital on August 18, despite the dire warnings triggered by a Vanity Fair article in which writer Lynn Hirschberg suggested that Courtney had used smack during her pregnancy. The repercussions thundered round the world, throwing up erroneous reports that the baby was born a heroin addict, blighting the reputations of both Courtney and Kurt (who was in the same hospital, yet again detoxing, when his daughter arrived) and colouring the public's future expectations of Nirvana. The whole controversy eventually led to Frances being taken into care for a while and to an enormous hostility towards the press from the Cobains.

Kurt and Courtney were eventually granted custody of Frances Bean by the beginning of 1993, when Kurt gushed over his family and seemed happier than ever, saying, "It's more important than anything else in the whole world. Playing music is what I do – my family is what I am," adding, "two years ago, I wouldn't even have considered having a child. I used to say that a person who would bring a child into this life now is selfish.

But I try to be optimistic, and things do look like they're getting a little bit better - just the way communication has progressed in the past ten years. MTV, whether its the evil corporate ogre or not, has played a part in raising consciousness."

His relationship with Love was also a sincere one, as he showed anger at being constantly compared to rock and roll hedonists Sid and Nancy, "To assume that we're just the same because we did heroin for a while - it's pretty offensive to be expected to be like that." He declared that he was "more attracted to Courtney than I've ever been toward a person before."

Reflecting on the furore, Kurt said "Courtney was honest about the heroin excursion we went on for a few months," Kurt reported. "Then Courtney found herself pregnant, realised she was pregnant and had a drug problem, and got off drugs. It's as simple as that." He added, "I'm just so tired of talking about this. We have to live with the results of this one article every fucking day. It's something we have to deal with all the time."

Even after the Vanity Fair article was circulating, and rumours of dissension within the Nirvana rank's arose, Kurt stood up for Courtney, and was honest about the trouble that had gone on between her and the band. He said, "There was article in the [British music magazine] NME that was nothing but an 'expose' on Courtney fucking up Nirvana and making us come close to breaking up. It's pretty frightening to find that an article like that can be written by a friend of yours. It makes it hard to trust anybody. Krist and Dave liked Courtney before I even liked Courtney. During that time, I knew that I liked her a lot, but I wouldn't admit it. She and Dave were really good friends - I shouldn't say this, but they almost wanted to get together for a time. When we were on tour in Europe, some of our shows collided with Hole shows, and Courtney would hang out on the bus with us, and Krist and Courtney were really good friends. And it hasn't changed at all."

Yet another feud began in April of 1992, this time with music magazine Rolling Stone, as Cobain became more and more frustrated with the media scrutiny he was under, and the perceived coolness of the band taking attention away from the music once again. "Rolling Stone sucks," he said, "has always sucked, and still sucks just because they have a hip band on their cover. We're not as cool and hip as everyone thinks. Having us on the cover isn't going to make Rolling Stone any cooler." He then continued with, "I have to learn to detour my thoughts and what I say in order to stop someone from saying I'm a hypocrite. That was the Rolling Stone debate: 'Corporate magazines suck, but you're still on the cover.' Well, of course! It's a joke. Get over it."

Within two weeks, Nirvana was back in England, where 'Lithium' had just enjoyed a Number 11 chart placing, to headline a rain-lashed, marshy Reading Festival on August 30. Kurt - tilting at rumours that he wouldn't turn up because he'd OD'd - appeared in a wheelchair wearing a hospital gown and a blonde wig belonging to Everett True, who also pushed him onstage. Cobain mimed a painful climb out of the chair, sang a line from U2's 'One', and fell to the floor. There was a sudden silence and then, realising that it was a put-on, the mud-spattered hordes went crazy.

Ben Thompson, reviewing for the Independent On Sunday, stated alliteratively: "The set which follows confounds carpers and crushes curmudgeons... No one lucky enough to have seen Nirvana do 'All Apologies' on this magical night will ever forget it."

True wrote: "It was obvious the band were out to have a good time. And fuck, so they did - in fact, the show was so superior to any others they played during 1992, it was like another band altogether. It was like it was 1990 again, and the Olympia trio didn't have a care in the world... they were not rock Gods, but three ordinary dudes out to have a fucking blast. This was the last truly great show I saw them play as a trio."

In America, 'Lithium' only made it to Number 64, but Nirvana gave it another outing when they appeared at the MTV Video Music Awards on September 9. Cobain had initially wanted to play the newly written 'Rape Me' - later to be featured both as a single and on the 1993 album In Utero. MTV was naturally appalled at the idea, and insisted the band play 'Smells Like Teen Spirit', but eventually agreed that they could play 'Lithium' instead. When Kurt began their performance he strummed the first few bars of 'Rape Me', almost having the show pulled off air, before lurching into 'Lithium'.

Over the autumn months, they played a short string of gigs. There was a concert at Portland Meadows Racetrack in aid of a gay rights campaign on September 10, where the band was reportedly off colour. Helmet's Page Hamilton told Carrie Borzillo: "Kurt was out of tune and he sounded whiny. Backstage, he's kind of slouched back and was a scrawny little guy and he just looked sickly. It didn't have anything to do with heroin, that certainly didn't help him, but he just looked like he wasn't healthy anyway."

The band was back on form the next night at another benefit show, this time at the Seattle Center Coliseum, in support of the Washington Music Industry Coalition, opposing censorship. Charles R. Cross viewed Nirvana's rip-roaring performance as "Kurt's 'Fuck you' to the critics", who by now were querying his state of health and his ability to keep up the good work. "This was his hometown, and from the first moment it's completely rocking," said Cross. "It was the resurrection of Kurt Cobain in Seattle, really." Gillian G Gaar told Everett True: "The entire floor was a big moshpit and the fans were just leaping around, leaping around, leaping around."

The last Nirvana gig of the year took place in Buenos Aires,

Argentina, on October 30 in front of 50,000 people. They refused to play 'Teen Spirit', while taunting the audience with its intro, and it was later said that only a spontaneous jam and an "amazing destruction sequence" at the end saved what had been a lacklustre performance.

Before this, they'd played a number of secret gigs: Kurt joined Sonic Youth and Mudhoney onstage in Valencia, California. Nirvana unexpectedly opened for Mudhoney at Bellingham, Washington and in Seattle. Kurt announced: "We just wanted to know what it felt like to be an alternative band in a nightclub again."

The fourth and final single from Nevermind - "In Bloom" - stalled at Number 28 in the British chart.

Perhaps as a reaction to the commercial sheen of Nevermind, Nirvana next released a compilation of rarities - demos, B-sides, out-takes and BBC radio sessions - . Incesticide in the December.

Cobain said of the album that, "Most of the stuff on Incesticide should have come out before Bleach, actually. But we did feel a little bit of pressure, a little bit of intimidation, by the whole Seattle scene because everyone was so heavily into this retro '70s thing," even going so far as to compare Nirvana to both the Knack and Kajagoogoo. "I'm not saying we're a punk rock band," he continued. "I'm saying we're a new wave band. But there were new wave bands that sold nine million copies. Like the Knack. All kinds of stuff like that. Kajagoogoo, whoever."

Rolling Stone once again awarded Nirvana three out of five, with writer Grant Alden stating: "Nirvana was a great band before Nevermind topped the charts. Incesticide is a reminder of that and - maybe more important - proof of Nirvana's ability, on occasion, to fail. The unpolished forces at work and sometimes in conflict within the band are plainly exposed, as is a broader and rougher range of sounds, styles and interests."

In his liner notes, Cobain stuck up for Courtney (by now

under constant attack by the press) as "a supreme example of dignity, ethics and honesty" and for himself, offering "a big fuck you to those of you who have the audacity to claim that I'm so naive and stupid that I would allow myself to be taken advantage of and manipulated".

The liner notes were also rather telling with regard to the band's thoughts on their new mainstream appeal: "If you're a racist, a sexist, a homophobe, we don't want you to buy our records." Still, in spite of this, the album managed to climb to number 39 in the U.S. charts and reached number 14 in the UK, as it contained various fan favourites such as 'Sliver' and 'Aneurysm', and accessible covers of songs by Scottish punks the Vaselines, and Cobain's personal favourites, Devo.

Incesticide reached Number 14 in the UK, and 39 in the States.

Nirvana began 1993 with a couple of stadium gigs in Brazil under the banner of "Hollywood Rocks" appearing with L7, Red Hot Chili Peppers and Alice In Chains. The first show, on January 16, at the 80,000-capacity Morumbi Stadium in Sao Paulo, was the biggest show of their career. It's best remembered as the occasion of Nirvana's "mental breakdown", which saw them attempting a "secret set" of unlikely songs by Duran Duran, Kim Wilde, Queen and Terry Jacks, whose 'Seasons In The Sun' was a Cobain favourite. The massive audience responded with silence, before the band trashed the entire stage.

The second of these shows took place at the Apotoese Stadium, Rio, a week later. Despite the guest appearance of the Chili Peppers' bassist Flea playing trumpet on 'Teen Spirit', the unveiling of a 17-minute 'Scentless Apprentice' and the sight of Kurt in a lacy frock and Grohl in a bra, the general consensus was that Nirvana were even more disappointing than they'd been in Sao Paulo. They did much better in San Francisco, where they played a benefit concert for Bosnian Rape Victims. Held at the Cow Palace on April 9 and also featuring The Breeders, L7 and Disposable Heroes of Hiphoprisy, the fund-raiser had been organised by Krist Novoselic, who had visited his homeland at the beginning of the year and heard terrible stories of what was befalling women there.

Everett True reported on the gig for Melody Maker: "I love Nirvana for 'Rape Me', tonight's opener... I love them for putting on tonight's show... the humanity at the core... I love Nirvana for Kurt's peerless way with a pop melody... for their encore, which is longer than their set used to be, for songs like 'Breed', 'Territorial Pissings' and 'Floyd The Barber', which still roar and buzz as they did before... for the way they don't play 'In Bloom' and 'Polly', thus avoiding the two songs that have the most potential for horrendous lighter-waving and clap-alongs, but still play 'Lithium' and 'Teen Spirit', because to have done otherwise would have been childishly churlish..."

By this time, they'd recorded their final studio album, In Utero, travelling to Minneapolis in February for 10 days' work with Steve Albini. They went into Pachyderm Studios in St Cloud on Valentine's Day.

Albini was most commonly known for his work on the Pixies' highly influential long-player Surfer Rosa, as well as work with such other indie rock acts as the Breeders, Big Black, and the Jesus Lizard - the band with which Nirvana had just released a split single through Touch & Go Records.

The sessions with Albini were extremely productive, and the embryonic version of Nirvana's third and final studio album was recorded and mixed in just two weeks. This was in stark contrast to the months spent recording and mixing for their breakthrough album, Nevermind. Initially Cobain was very happy with Albini and the production:

"The main reason we recorded the new album with Steve Albini is he is able to get a sound that sounds like the band is in a room no bigger than the one we're in now. In Utero doesn't sound like it's been recorded in a hall, or that it's trying to sound larger than life. It's very in-your-face and real."

Many saw the decision to bring in Albini to produce the album as a deliberate move by Nirvana to alienate, or at least distance themselves from, some of their more mainstream fans who knew little or nothing of such obscure or experimental punk bands as the Vaselines and Mudhoney, who Nirvana saw as their forbears. Albini had previously produced raw, unpolished-sounding albums. One song in particular, ironically titled 'Radio Friendly Unit Shifter', featured long periods of shrill feedback, and all the members of the band showed great excitement about its release.

Krist divulged that, "I really want people to hear this record. I get really idealistic about it. There's a lot of 'alternative' bands out there, and their music would basically fit in the repertoire of Springsteen or some serious mainstream stuff. They're marketed as alternative, and they're confusing people."

"Oh man," Kurt added, "that's why I'm so excited about this record. I actually want to promote this record, not for the sake of selling records, but because I'm more proud of this record than anything I've ever done. We've finally achieved the sound that I've been hearing in my head forever."

In fact, there was a time when In Utero (originally, and somewhat prophetically, entitled I Hate Myself And I Want To Die) was expected to be a relative flop after the commercial success of Nevermind. Fans and music industry executives alike had convinced themselves that the pressure of following up the 10-million-record-selling Nevermind, combined with Kurt's alleged drug problems, had left him in a creative funk, and his comments before the albums release, relating to his lack of lyrics, only fuelled the fire. The songs that did eventually emerge however, took a more thematic turn, as lyrics showing a fascination with female anatomy and the human body came to the fore, as well as songs based more upon other art forms rather than just the trappings of Kurt Cobain's head. "There are more songs on this album that are thematic," he said, "that are actually about something rather than just pieces of poetry. Like, 'Scentless Apprentice' is about the book, Perfume, by Patrick Süskind. I don't think I've ever written a song based on a book before." Whether this was Cobain branching out or merely retreating further into himself was a major bone of contention, however.

The aim this time was a rough and very aggressive production, and they achieved it so well that Geffen ruffled Albini's feathers by demanding some cosmetic changes including louder vocals. "Geffen and the band's management hate the record," Albini said at the time, adding that he had "no faith this record will be released." Cobain's story was different however.

"There has been no pressure from our record label to change the tracks we did with Albini," he said in a prepared statement, adding, "We have 100-percent control of our music."

Specifically, the band said that they had thought there was something wrong with the record very early on and after listening to it over a week-long period had come to the conclusion that the bass levels were too low and that the vocals were lost in the mix. 'Heart-Shaped Box' and 'All Apologies' came under particularly close scrutiny, as Cobain had felt that they hadn't sounded "perfect." He pointed out that this was his record - the record that meant the most to him – and that everything needed to sound exactly as he had heard it in his head. Long-time R.E.M. producer Scott Litt was brought in to help remix the two songs, with Cobain adding additional vocals and instrumentation, as the band strived for perfection.

There were some people at Geffen who would not have released the album had they had their way, their hopes for another

Nevermind instantly demolished with one listen to In Utero, which they reputedly deemed "un-releasable". Presumably large slices of humble pie were served and digested when the album charted at Number One in both Britain and the US although, in the meantime, the controversy made its way into the Chicago Tribune and from there into the international press.

The album was actually a testament to Cobain's uncertain temperament as he struggled to get a grip on the reality that he was in the biggest rock act in the world at that time. Dave Grohl, in particular, found himself on the receiving end of some highly contrasting ideas surrounding In Utero. He revealed that, "I don't think I've ever told anyone this, but there were times when Kurt was really unhappy with the way I played drums. I could hear him talking about how much he thought I sucked. But he'd never say it to me. If I'd confront him about it – 'Is there a problem? If you want me to leave, just ask' - he'd say, 'No, no, no.' Most of that happened later, around In Utero. That's when I think Kurt became unhappy with what was happening with the band."

However, only a couple of weeks later Kurt had seemingly made a complete about-face, as Grohl added, "I came home and turned on my message machine and had a message from Kurt that said, 'Y'know, I was just sitting here listening to In Utero, and your drumming is so awesome. You did such a great job!' I was like, 'Wow!'"

Still, this contradictory behaviour had always been present, even from the earliest days of the band, as Krist himself attested, when he detailed Kurt's inclination for loneliness in an interview following his death in 1994. "I called Kurt 'The Windmill,'" laughed Novoselic, "because he would say something, then five minutes later he'd completely contradict himself. And he would laugh; because he knew he did it. There would be times when he really wanted to be a rock star, and there were times when he hated it. He just couldn't figure it out."

Krist then added, "He was living in this tiny apartment in Olympia, Washington by himself. He was always cranking out art: - this new painting, this new sculpture or some weird collage. He liked to be left alone. Then he got sucked out of there, and he was put on this pedestal."

It was this difficulty in coping with the adulation that both he and the band were receiving that some say drove Cobain to his eventual demise, as he consistently tried to downplay the band's mainstream position in the run-up to the release of In Utero.

"I don't see much of a change, personally," he said. "I've said this a million times, and I'm kind of tired of saying it, but we're a new wave band and that's what happened with new wave. Punk rock was the revolution. It was the groundbreaking thing, and then all these punk rock bands started making really tame palatable music with punk rock fashion. It entered the mainstream and became popular for a while. It was a fad, and that's the way I look at alternative music. Every once in a while I'll look at the Billboard charts and I just go, 'Crap, crap, crap,' just like I always have. Except for R.E.M., and I mean they totally deserve to be on top 40, but I really can't think of any bands that are on top 40 right now that I like, personally."

In March, the Cobains moved from LA to a rented house in Seattle. During the early summer, the truth about Cobain's heroin use and turbulent domestic life burst into the open when the emergency services were called to the couple's home on two occasions; once to break up a violent argument between the pair which ended with Kurt being thrown into the local jail for a couple of hours accused of assaulting Courtney, an allegation both vigorously denied; and on the other occasion, to rush him to hospital suffering a heroin overdose. This all made headlines across the world, but it was not Cobain's only OD that year. He continued shooting smack and on July 23, he was said to have actually died with a needle in his arm before being revived by a frantic Courtney and the family nanny. Only a few hours later, Kurt was onstage with Nirvana at a one-off New York gig at the Roseland Ballroom as part of the city's New Music Seminar.

This was a brave gig for the band, and not just because Kurt had so recently risen from the dead. They'd decided to augment the line-up with a second guitarist, the former Exploited heavyweight Big John Duncan, who was also one of Cobain's guitar techs, and Lori Goldston a classically trained cellist. Nirvana started the set with two unknown songs from In Utero, 'Serve The Servants' and 'Scentless Apprentice', before roaring into such familiar fare as 'Breed', 'Lithium', 'Rape Me', 'Aneurysm' and 'Territorial Pissings'. But it was when they had the audacity to introduce an acoustic section that the audience, until now raucously on the band's side, demonstrably disapproved.

Jon Savage reported in The Observer: "When it becomes clear that Nirvana are not going to rock, an abyss opens between the group and the audience: you can hear it as the buzz from the crowd threatens to drown out the acoustic instruments."

They laughed and talked loudly over 'Polly', 'Dumb' and

'Where Did You Sleep Last Night', ignoring Nirvana's attempts to bring subtlety and imagination to the performance. Kurt later told Q magazine he thought it "very rude".

The band walked off to a deafening silence and then - amazingly, given their temperament - returned to give the punters a noisy 'Teen Spirit'. Savage saw the whole thing as "a total punk rock show; a bitter, dogged stand-off between the group's insistence on doing what they want and the audience's expectations of what they should do."

He asked: "How can the members of Nirvana retain their integrity, which is very important to them, in a situation which demands constant compromise? How can they sing from the point of view of an outsider now that they're in a privileged position?" These would have been the issues troubling Kurt Cobain in those increasingly rare moments when he wasn't anaesthetised by heroin. Meeting Kurt in person, Savage found him "courteous, intelligent, quiet".

In an interview with The Face a few days later, Kurt memorably stated: "I've been suicidal all my life. I just don't want to die now. Having a child and being in love is the only thing I feel I've been blessed with."

There was one other gig that summer, at Seattle's King Theatre on August 6. It was a benefit to raise money for an investigation into the death of The Gits' lead singer Mia Zapata who'd been raped, strangled and killed on the street. This gig was Nirvana's last as a three-piece.

Despite the crowd reactions at the Roseland Ballroom, the band retained Lori Goldston - and the concept of an acoustic section - for the In Utero tour beginning in October 1993. Big John had played his one and only gig with Nirvana, but they recruited another guitarist, Pat Smear, from legendary LA punk band The Germs.

Pat, a hardcore hero, was born Georg Ruthenberg to mixed-race parents. His mother, an opera singer, was of African-American/Cherokee descent and his father, an inventor, was a German Jewish immigrant. Pat's lifelines were unusual to say the least, living in a Jesus commune at an early age and later attending a special Innovative Program school in Santa Monica for teenagers who were unsuited to the conventional education system. There he met Darby Crash, with whom he founded The Germs. Smear's influences ranged from Alice Cooper to David Bowie, from Yes's Steve Howe to British punk. By the time he was invited to join Nirvana, who were all younger than himself, he had appeared as a punk rocker in films such as Blade Runner.

"It was pretty intimidating," Smear said of his appointment to Nirvana in a 2002 internet interview with Rasmus Holmen. "It took a while to get over the feeling that I didn't deserve it."

"Pat has worked out great from day one," Kurt himself remarked. "In addition to being one of the my closest friends, Pat has found a niche in our music that complements what was already there, without forcing any major changes."

"There were times when the room was lit up with energy and happiness," Dave Grohl later added, "and there were times when the vibe was like the fucking plague. The last year, being in that band was rough. There was a whole lot of dark shit going on. At that point I was living this wonderful, healthy life outside the band, but when I'd enter a band environment that all changed. It wasn't a lot of fun. But when Pat Smear joined the band, it changed everything. We went from being fucking sulking dirt bags to kids again. It changed our world. He's the sweetest person in the world. He became really close with Kurt. There was laughter."

Before the tour began, however, Nirvana instructed tour manager Alex MacLeod to fire their loyal friend and sound engineer Craig Montgomery, on the grounds that they were unhappy with their recent recording for Saturday Night Live. This was "pretty devastating" for Montgomery, who had helped with but was not in charge of the sound for the TV show.

Nirvana was taking to the road on the back of yet more chart success. 'Heart-Shaped Box' had been a Number Five hit in the UK in September, and In Utero followed a couple of weeks later, topping the charts on either side of the Atlantic although not selling in anything like the quantities of Nevermind, which was now approaching sales of five million. By now Pearl Jam was overtaking Nirvana in popularity.

Despite the reservations of some of DGC's highest-ranking personnel, the critics loved In Utero and its perverse rawness. Rolling Stone's David Fricke awarded it four out of five stars. His review pulled no punches: "Never in the history of rock'n'roll overnight sensations has an artist, with the possible exception of John Lennon, been so emotionally overwhelmed by his sudden good fortune, despised it with such devilish vigor and exorcised his discontent on record with such bristling, bull's-eye candor. In Utero is rife with gibes - some hilariously droll, others viciously direct - at life in the post-Nevermind fast lane, at the money-changers who milked the grunge tit dry in record time and at the bandwagon sheep in the mosh pit who never caught on to the desperate irony of 'Here we are now, entertain us'."

Fricke loved the "ravishing clutter" and he concluded: "In Utero is a lot of things - brilliant, corrosive, enraged and thoughtful, most of them all at once. But more than anything, it's a triumph of the will."

Ben Thompson, in the Independent On Sunday, had some criticisms. Although he seemed to like the "blood and guts - 'I wish I could eat your cancer', 'Her milk is my shit', etc - a lot of shouting, and some major-league perversity", he complained of self-indulgence and the odd "bum steer". He decided that "for all that, In Utero is beautiful far more often than it is ugly and the best moments here - the lovely, plaintive 'All Apologies', the lustrous 'Dumb' ("I think I'm dumb or maybe just happy") - have an uplifting quality that actually goes beyond Nevermind."

Dave Grohl put it simply to Q's Phil Sutcliffe: "This album sounds like Nirvana!" Sutcliffe responded that it "isn't the easy-listening option".

For some it certainly made uneasy listening. Mega chain store Wal-Mart refused to carry the album on the grounds that it was far too controversial for their "family-orientated store outlook," citing the song title 'Rape Me' and Cobain's plastic foetus collage on the album's artwork as their main concerns. The band acted to accommodate, compiling a version of the album with so-called clean artwork and re-titling 'Rape Me' to 'Waif Me'. Again the band might have been on dodgy ground, but they justified what might have been seen as pandering to big business by insisting that they were thinking of small-town fans who had no other local music stores and were forced to buy their music at Wal-Mart.

Their first major arena tour - which was mostly but not completely sold out - started in Phoenix, Arizona, at the Veterans Memorial Coliseum on October 18. Novoselic described the opening night to MTV News: "With all the lighters out there, it felt like we were doing Aerosmith's 'Dream On' or something." Kurt was becoming nervous of the crowds, who "immediately started grabbing for me, trying to rip my flesh off for souvenirs... all they know how to do is tear people apart".

There were some negative reviews. Robert Hilburn noted in the LA Times that "the pacing was sluggish and the playing at times reflected the tentativeness of learning to work together onstage". USA Today declared: "Creative anarchy deteriorated into bad performance art as the band overindulged a tendency toward wilful chaos."

By now, Kurt and Pat Smear were travelling in a different tour bus to everyone else. The original camaraderie, the essential punk egalitarianism, had degenerated into separation and a reported tendency on Cobain's part to pick on Dave Grohl. A lot of people around the band predicted that it couldn't carry on for much longer.

Eventually, Nirvana got into their musical stride, although they weren't consistently brilliant. For every fun night such as the Akron, Ohio, show where they all dressed up for Halloween, and the music was described by every reviewer as "amazing", there were shockers. At the second of two gigs at Chicago's Aragon Ballroom, on October 25, Nirvana was booed by their audience for what was lambasted by Rolling Stone as "a real stinker". Geffen's Jim Merlis told Carrie Borzillo: "It was a mess. Probably the worst show of the tour. I think that part of it was because Kurt was really nervous about the Rolling Stone interview that he was doing after the show." In Detroit, someone hit Kurt on the head with a shoe.

Jim Sullivan of the Boston Globe, reviewing the Springfield, Massachusetts, performance, was sure he heard "the cries of an over-stressed human being". The New York Times' Peter Watrous said of Nirvana's Coliseum show: "There's no escape from the pop mechanism, and it seems as if Mr Cobain hasn't quite come to terms with it." Simon Reynolds, reviewing the same show for Melody Maker, confirmed that Nirvana had "truly connected with America's rock heartland... the Great White Hopeless" and said of Kurt: "As he continues to squirm excruciatingly on all the jagged contradictions of turning rebellion into $$$$, I'm sure there will be great songs to come but, Jesus Christ, I wouldn't want to be in his shoes for all the pennyroyal tea in China."

As Krist Novoselic remarked to Musician magazine: "It used to be an adventure. And now it's a circus."

In an interview given at the start of February, Cobain cited frustration as the reason for the band's boredom.

"I have," he said, "lots of ideas and musical ambitions that have nothing to do with this mass conception of 'grunge' that has been force-fed to the record-buying public for the past few years. Whether I will be able to do everything I want to do as part of Nirvana remains to be seen. To be fair, I also know that both Krist and Dave have musical ideas that may not work within the context of Nirvana. We're all tired of being labelled. You can't imagine how stifling it is."

He added, "I'm extremely proud of what we've accomplished together. Having said that, however, I don't know how long we can continue as Nirvana without a radical shift in direction."

Things weren't going swimmingly, then. Steve Turner from Mudhoney, who'd been supporting on some of the dates, revealed to Everett True: "That tour with Nirvana was horrible. It was the least fun we'd ever had. It was heartbreaking how fucked-up their organisation was. Kurt was miserable and secluded, it was so horribly sad. . ."

True - who guested with Nirvana as The Legend! at various gigs including Washington, DC and New York - documents this period differently: "Oddly, almost all my memories of Nirvana live in 1993 are happy ones."

At the tail end of the tour the band was supported by The Meat Puppets, a band that Kurt loved. Since brothers Curt and Cris Kirkwood, the creative force in the band, were his idols, Kurt convinced them to play with Nirvana in their upcoming performance for MTV's Unplugged series, which was due to be filmed in New York during a break from the tour; and so the ensemble began rehearsing for the show. The rehearsals went well, and it seemed as though it might be a stress-free interaction with MTV, something that was fairly alien to Nirvana. On the actual day, however, it was clear that Kurt was suffering from

withdrawal, and he needed something to help him before he could perform. The MTV crew supplied him with everything they could think of, from fried chicken to Valium, until a stage hand Kurt had organised arrived with exactly what he needed. And with that he was ready to play.

'All Apologies' was released as a single, in the UK only, on November 9. Everett's Melody Maker review swooned: "It's the most supremely resigned, supremely weary fuck you to the outside world I've heard this year. 'All Apologies' has the most gorgeous, aching tune, an emotionally draining ennui. Every time I hear Kurt break into that line, 'Choking on the ashes of our enemies', I grow close to tears..." The single reached Number 32 - Nirvana's lowest entry since 'In Bloom'.

On November 18, Nirvana recorded their most powerful TV performance, one take for MTV Unplugged. Released after Kurt's death, these songs in their acoustic form took on an almost unbearably poignant significance. As Ben Thompson would later put it in Mojo magazine: "Listening to this record for the first time is like having a picture of a friend who has just died and not being sure if you want to look at it so soon." Joined by the Kirkwoods, Nirvana played haunting versions of The Meat Puppet's 'Plateau', 'Oh Me' and 'Lake Of Fire'. They also covered The Vaselines' 'Jesus Doesn't Want Me For A Sunbeam', on which Novoselic returned to the accordion, the first instrument he had learned, David Bowie's 'The Man Who Sold The World' and Leadbelly's 'Where Did You Sleep Last Night' as well as leafing through their own back pages: 'About A Girl', 'Come As You Are', 'Pennyroyal Tea', 'Dumb', 'Polly', 'On A Plain', 'Something In The Way' and 'All Apologies' were all given the bare bones treatment.

Novoselic said later: "We put a lot of work into pulling that together. Kurt was really happy after that show - and relieved. He did such a great job. Everybody did such a great job."

After another MTV performance on December 13, for Live And Loud, when the band noticeably rediscovered their old fiery intensity, the tour carried on through Christmas, and Nirvana played their last-ever American concerts at the Seattle Center Arena on January 7 and 8, 1994. At this point, Lori Goldston left the band, to be replaced by the corset-wearing Melora Creager from New York cello trio Rasputina.

Pausing only to buy a new family home - a million-dollar mansion in a rich district of Seattle - in mid-January, and to nip into the Robert Lang Studios in Shoreline, Washington for three days with Krist and Dave, Kurt packed his bags, waved goodbye to Courtney and flew to Europe with the band. A darkly grim atmosphere settled around them on this tour. Kurt was depressed. He didn't wish to be on the road at all. He was hardly speaking to his bandmates. His throat was seizing up, and he developed laryngitis and bronchitis. He was withdrawing from heroin but taking morphine. He was upset at being lauded as a junkie icon. He was convinced that Courtney was cheating on him. According to The True Story, he was "lost in a defeatist, sullen daze". Melora told Carrie Borzillo: "After every show, Kurt would just lie down on a couch and just wait to leave." She described him as "seriously and dangerously depressed".

Nirvana struggled on for a month. As had so often happened in Europe, they then called off the last two dates of this leg of the tour, in Germany. Their last performance was at Munich's Terminal Einz on March 1 1994. Kurt went to Rome where Courtney joined him. It wasn't quite the romantic reunion he'd envisaged. In the early hours of the next morning, March 4, he attempted suicide by swallowing up to 60 Rohypnol pills, but was saved when Courtney awoke in the nick of time.

The suicide attempt was initially reported as an accidental overdose, as a doctor told an assembled group of news and music journalists that Cobain had reacted badly to a combination of the tranquilliser and champagne. The tour was cancelled and many devoted fans around the world were in despair over the reports of Cobain's behaviour.

As he himself repeatedly insisted, however, he had never wanted that lifestyle, and the idea of being a role model confused him considerably. He mused that "there's no one in rock and roll right now who's a relevant example of a spokesperson for anything."

He also hated the constant scrutiny he was under, especially the-drug abuse rumours. "I have people checking up on me all the time," he stated, "especially because of the heroin rumours. That's been blown out of proportion so severely that I'm constantly harassed at airports and immigration all the time. And the cops - I get pulled over whenever they recognise me, and they search my car." More than anything, Kurt just wanted to be left alone.

The rest of the proposed tour was cancelled and the band returned to the US to prepare for Lollapalooza, a festival that everyone wanted to play; apart from Kurt, who would have been happy to retreat to his house and his drug addiction, were it not for the tension mounting at home between him and Courtney. Their regular arguments, and his constant drug abuse, made home life for the Cobains anything but peaceful.

By mid-March Kurt was refusing everything the band was offering him. He said no to touring, to Lollapalooza and to rehearsing: Nirvana had effectively split up. Krist and Dave gave up trying to get through to him. He had failed to heed anything anyone said to him since his suicide attempt in Rome, and his refusal to attend practice sessions was a final confirmation for the others—the onus was on them to decide what to do next.

Kurt stayed a recluse for the next month during which he saw Krist twice; on the first occasion he seemed too spaced out to realise what was going on, and then bummed a lift from his old friend to try to find drugs. On the second occasion, Krist forcefully escorted him to Seattle airport. Once there the two fought, as Kurt tried to flee, eventually managing to wriggle and kick his way free from his friend's grasp. As he ran away he screamed a final 'fuck you' to his band-mate, and then was gone.

On March 18, the police had to talk the troubled Nirvana frontman out of suicide once again, after he locked himself in a room threatening to kill himself. Courtney Love, along with Nirvana's management team, organised an intervention program that resulted in Kurt's admission to the Exodus Recovery Centre in L.A. on March 30, 1994, but he escaped yet again, returning to Seattle on April 1. Although he was spotted in various locations around the city, none of those closest to Cobain knew of his exact whereabouts; Love hired a private investigator to track him down and Cobain's mother filed a 'missing person's' report on April 4th. On April 8th, a workman hired to install a security lighting system at the Cobain's home discovered Kurt lying dead; a shotgun, which he had apparently used to kill himself on or around April 5th , lay by his side He was just twenty seven years old.

"The thing was," Grohl recalled, "I don't know if I've ever told anyone this - somebody had actually told me that Kurt had died before he died. They told me he had died in Rome, so I started grieving when he had his OD in Rome." He added, "The time leading up to his death was really strange. He disappeared. He just seemed like he wanted to get away. He bailed. I honestly did not think he was going to kill himself. I just thought he was on someone's floor in Olympia, listening to albums or something."

"It's so hard to remember everything," Grohl went on to muse. "I wish I'd kept a journal. I wish I'd taken pictures. I felt as confused then as I do now about the whole thing."

Several Nirvana albums have been released following Cobain's death. The first came out in November 1994, with the release of the band's eerily morbid and subdued performance in New York for MTV Unplugged. This was swiftly followed by a video documenting much of the Nevermind tour, mostly compiled by Cobain himself, but completed by Grohl and Novoselic following his death.

It was Kurt's belief in creative control that he must be remembered for most; he only ever wanted to be able to write and express himself. It was everything else that came with his position that he struggled with so much.

"Writing," he'd once said, "is the one part that is not a job; it's expression. Photo shoots, interviews... that's the real job part." Then he added that "the real core of any tenderness or rage is tapped the very second that a song is written. In a sense, I'm only re-creating the purity of that particular emotion every time I play that particular song."

In the wake of Cobain's death, there was much legal wrangling between Courtney Love, Dave Grohl, and Krist Novoselic. Grohl - now, of course, a member of Foo Fighters - and Novoselic - who went on to form Sweet 75, and later Eyes Adrift - organised a box set of Nirvana rarities which was due to be released in September 2001 to coincide with the 10th anniversary of the release of Nevermind. Shortly before the release date, however, Love filed an injunction to stop the box set coming out, claiming that Cobain's former bandmates were only looking after their own personal interests, and didn't have the band's legacy at heart.

Much of the dispute centred around a single unreleased song, 'You Know You're Right', taken from the band's final studio recording. The two former Nirvana bandmates planned on including the track on the rarities set. Love, however, had other ideas, arguing that the song was more important than that and should be included instead on a single-disc greatest-hits compilation. In the end Love got her way, and The Best Of... was released in late 2002, followed by the box set's eventual release in November 2004, the band's third posthumous release.

The enquiries into Cobain's death still rumble on to this day, with many suggesting that his death was not suicide but murder. Tom Grant, for example, the private investigator once employed by Courtney Love, is adamant that Cobain's death was a homicide, citing the official toxicology report, which claims his heroin level was three times the lethal dosage at the time of his death and arguing that Cobain wouldn't have been able to pull the trigger of a shotgun with such a huge amount of heroin in his system.

Other private investigations have been carried out by film-makers and journalists alike. However, while the murder conspiracy theories remain ever-popular amongst a group of hardened Nirvana fans, most still generally accept the official verdict of death by self-inflicted gunshot wound, pointing to Cobain's clinical depression, persistent drug addiction, and hand-written suicide note as conclusive proof in the whole sordid matter. People also cite Novoselic's and Grohl's silence on the matter as proof that they also believe it was a cut-and-dry suicide. As Ben Thompson, journalist for the independent On Sunday, so aptly put it, "The very otherworldliness and individuality which made him such a compelling figure rendered him incapable of coping with the fame these qualities brought him"

Still, amongst all the controversy, it only seems right to let Cobain have the last say, as he simply and resonantly put it in an early interview, "It's not that I'm trying to dictate; it's just that I am afforded a certain platform on which I can express my views. At the very least, I always get the last word." In this case, at least, he certainly did.

EPILOGUE

Krist and Dave were now part of the continuing development of the grunge genre, as they took on new projects. Dave invited Krist to be a part of his new band, The Foo Fighters; but Krist was concerned that having the two of them in the same band would be seen as a sequel to Nirvana, or an attempt to cash in.

Instead, he went on to take a more political stance, campaigning for changes to US legislation and forming JAMPAC (the Joint Artists and Musicians Political Action Committee), an organisation which campaigned on a number of issues, including the repealing of the 1985 Teen Dance Ordinance, a Seattle law which severely restricted the rights of young people to attend gigs. Even outside a band format, Novoselic was intent on making sure fans could hear the music that they wanted to hear. In 2004 he published his first book, Of Grunge and Government: Let's Fix This Broken Democracy.

Krist has been in several bands since Kurt's death, and is currently a member of Flipper, a California-based punk band. The Foo Fighters are still going strong, and Dave has managed to make a name for himself outside of Nirvana.

Well over decade since the band ended, Nirvana's influence on rock music is undeniable. They stretched musical boundaries and expanded horizons. Grunge was about the underdogs flexing their muscles, and reminding the world that, when united, they demanded attention. Since the grunge explosion, fashion and music have been dictated by what those previously sidelined have to say, and record companies no longer underestimate underground successes. Nirvana empowered those who had previously seemed unimportant. This surely is the most enduring part of their considerable legacy.

TRACK-BY-TRACK ANALYSIS

This track-by-track review of Nirvana's vast recorded back catalogue from 1988 right through to 2005 aims to provide a clear, concise, and unbiased evaluation of each of their songs and albums. Some songs are included more than once, such as of those on a live album, a compilation album or that were singles, as well as being on an original studio album; and this is clearly indicated.

With a focus both on UK releases and a number of important releases from Japan, the USA, and other parts of the world, I have tried my best to be as thorough as possible.

As far as singles, live albums, and compilation albums are concerned I have decided not to annotate each track, reserving fuller investigation for the original studio-based albums. When new tracks do appear on box sets, live albums, and the like, I have also annotated these tracks. Nirvana's penchant for covering the likes of Bowie, Leadbelly, and The Meat Puppets is also explored where I have felt it necessary.

Each song and album has been given a rating out of five as follows:

★ ★ ★ ★ ★ Essential
★ ★ ★ ★ Excellent
★ ★ ★ Good
★ ★ Average
★ Poor

As well as studio albums, singles, live albums and compilations, Nirvana also boasts a number of box sets, DVDs, and myriad bootlegs. Again, I have also included an overview of a number of these where I have deemed them important to their career.

LOVE BUZZ

(Single, November 1988)

Tracklisting: 'Love Buzz' / 'Big Cheese'

After a number of early false starts, the original incarnation of Nirvana - Kurt Cobain, Krist Novoselic, and Aaron Burckhard - are finally on record in 1987. Burckhard played at the band's very first live show in early 1988, but had been replaced by Chad Channing by the time this early single was released late in 1988. The sound on this Shocking Blue cover is harsh, and Channing's drumming basic, but it is Cobain's vocals combined with distorted guitars and Novoselic's driving bass line that make this limited edition, hand numbered, early 7" single well worth tracking down. "Can you feel my love buzz?"

Overall rating ★ ★

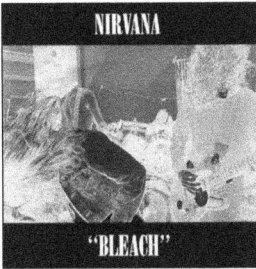

BLEACH

(Album, June 15 1989)

Tracklisting: 'Blew' / 'Floyd the Barber' / 'About a Girl' / 'School' / 'Love Buzz' / 'Paper Cuts' / 'Negative Creep' / 'Scoff' / 'Swap Meet' / 'Mr. Moustache' / 'Sifting' / 'Big Cheese' / 'Downer'

Blew ★ ★

A fairly solid opening to their first studio album kicks in with Novoselic playing a simplistic, repeated bass riff - completely unaccompanied - for the first seven seconds or so before the screech of Cobain's guitar feedback merges seamlessly into a mess of guitars and Channing's rather simplistic bashing of the skins. Cobain's famed gravelly voice makes an appearance during the chorus and bridge, with a sneering, slurred style employed for the verses. While simplistic lyrically, it's not a bad statement of intent to kick off this uber-grungey record.

Floyd the Barber ★ ★

Recorded early in 1988 with Dale Crover of the Melvins on drums, 'Floyd the Barber' is a whimsical song about small-town America. After Channing's Bleach sessions failed to live up to Crover's versions, this track is a remix of the original Crover recording and has a drum sound reminiscent of the Rolling Stone's 'My Obsession'. Another burst of guitar feedback takes us into the track, followed by a heavy, basic rhythm that eventually finds its place as a mid-tempo punk track. It is noteworthy lyrically, as Cobain introduces us to his dark sense of humour with, "Floyd breathes hard, I hear a zip, Pee-pee pressed against my lips." Has a somewhat weak verse, though.

About a Girl ★ ★ ★ ★ ★

Easily the most memorable song on Bleach, 'About a Girl' alone earns the album an extra star. Great verse, great chorus, great lyrics - even the weak production values seem to enhance this formidable track. Raw and sparse in comparison to Nevermind's material, 'About a Girl' displays the quiet/loud dynamic reminiscent of the Pixies and Dinosaur Jr.; a style Nirvana later made their own. Written by Cobain after an entire afternoon of listening to Meet the Beatles!, 'About a Girl' is probably one of the only traditional love songs he ever wrote. The laidback, discordant guitar in the verses provides welcome respite from the unabashed grunge of the rest of the album. It should come as no surprise that 'About a Girl' ranks in at number two in both the NME's and Q's "Greatest Ever Nirvana Songs."

School ★ ★ ★

This is a tongue-in-cheek tale written by Cobain about Sub Pop and the famed 'Seattle scene' of the time. According to Cobain, the song started out as something of a joke, but actually turned out to be an album highlight. A heavy, washed-out track with a solid riff accompanies Kurt repeating the mere 15-word lyrics of the song over and over and over again, as if a mantra, "Why won't you believe it / It's just my luck / No recess / You're in high school again."

Love Buzz ★ ★

This cover version of Shocking Blue's 1970s 'Love Buzz' differs lyrically from the original and is also mixed differently than the 1988 pre-Bleach single, missing the 10-second sound-collage intro Cobain put together for starters. This is a song that showcases Cobain's underplayed guitar skills, and proves to some extent that he was not just a voice-and-lyrics man. This is a solid cover that Nirvana made their own, creating the beginning of the Nirvana legend. A basic three-chord structure backs the vocals, omnipresent static and feedback rear their ugly head once again. It is a cover though, so it's difficult to give it much more than two stars as a Nirvana track.

Paper Cuts ★ ★

The Melvins' noteworthy influence on Nirvana's sound is particularly prevalent in this track, which partially based on the true story of a family in Aberdeen who kept their children locked up in a windowless room, only opening the door to feed them. The song also brings to the fore Cobain's feelings of alienation from the world, as he references the detachment he had from his mother, singing, "The lady whom I feel maternal love for / cannot look me in the eyes." Aside from that, this song is highly skip-able and has no real structure to speak of.

Negative Creep ★ ★ ★

Much-covered by metal bands such as Machine Head and Velvet Revolver, 'Negative Creep' shows off the band's punk-rock roots, though there is little hint of the band's later direction. The track begins with a chugging, metal-esque introduction before descending into a crescendo of noise, accompanied by Cobain's stream-of-consciousness lyrics. Full of passion and energy, it comes as no surprise that this track soon became a staple of Nirvana's live shows.

Scoff ★ ★

Cobain always cited Get The Knack by the Knack as one of the greatest pop albums of all time, and that is heard here with Channing's drum intro and a basic tempo that both owe a lot to the Knack's classic 'My Sharona'. It's most likely about Cobain's parents' disdain for his musical aspirations, with, "In your room I'm not older / In your eyes I'm not worth it." Scoff is an average track on an average Nirvana record.

Swap Meet ★

Along with 'Sifting', this track is one of the low points on the album. 'Swap Meet' is an album filler at best, and pretty poor at worst. It's very possible to believe the rumour that Cobain wrote most of the lyrics only three days before going into the studio. The weak production doesn't help much, either.

Mr. Moustache ★ ★

Mildly interestingly enough, it is one of the first alternative rock songs to have a title that cannot be found in its lyrics, which set a bit of a trend for the genre. The song is tolerable, but, thanks to the low production values, its a little too grungey. Cobain sings with urgency, bitterness, and an underlying longing for acceptance on the track. "Help me trust your mighty wisdom / Yes I eat cow / I am not proud." Once again his lyrics and heart save the day on this otherwise average track.

Sifting ★

One of the last songs to be written for the album, and it shows, as it almost feels rushed and just thrown in there for good measure. Cobain's lyrics, for once, falter here, although its worth reminding the listener that he was still relatively young and this was their first full-length studio album.

Big Cheese ★ ★

With vocals drenched in anger and aimed towards Jonathon Poneman, Nirvana's boss at Sub Pop, 'Big Cheese' originally appeared on the 'Love Buzz' single, and wasn't added to the record until Geffen re-released Bleach in September 1992. Filled with a couple of interesting tempo changes not really heard on other tracks, this interesting piece also has a lead guitar part with enough drive and shading to provide some more heaviness on an otherwise grunge-based record.

Downer ★ ★

Bleach closes with another song that begins with a repetitive bass riff before the rest of the band joins in. A catchy chorus with a quick, energetic beat save what is an otherwise derivative political song with not much else going for it. The verses are accompanied only by the bass riff, as Cobain sounds off in a fast-paced speech-song, filled with sarcasm and playfulness, an indicator of his general attitude and a taste of things to come.

Conclusion

Jack Endino, a producer seminal in the onset of the Seattle Sound, recorded Bleach in two separate sessions for only $750. The low production values, unfortunately, are all too evident. However, the album works as more than a sum of its separate parts, and real potential for the future was shown in two or three songs that stand out both lyrically and melodically. To fans of Nirvana it's a must-own; to others it's a raw mess of sound and noise. Final verdict? Could, and will do better.

Overall rating ★ ★

BLEW
(EP, December 1989)

Tracklisting: 'Blew' / 'Love Buzz' / 'Been a Son' / 'Stain'

A UK-only release in both 12" vinyl and CD formats on the Tupelo record label. 'Blew' and 'Love Buzz' were hijacked directly from Bleach, and although this is their first appearance on record, both versions of 'Been a Son' and 'Stain' appear on later releases, making this limited-edition EP one for collectors and enthusiasts only.

Overall rating ★ ★

SLIVER
(Single, September 1990)

Tracklisting: 'Sliver' / 'Dive' / 'About a Girl' (live, 1990) / 'Spank Thru' (live, 1990)

Catchy, and with groundings in pop punk, 'Sliver' came as a welcome release after almost a year of inactivity on the release front. Backed up by grunge-soaked track 'Dive', the two re-surfaced on Incesticide a few years later. Live versions of 'About a Girl' and 'Spank Thru' showcase the band's energy. A phone call between Novoselic and Jonathon Poneman of Sub Pop also provides an amusing side piece. Good stuff.

Overall rating ★ ★ ★

MOLLY'S LIPS / CANDY
(Split single with the Fluid, January 1991)

Tracklisting: 'Molly's Lips' / 'Candy' (by the Fluid)

This vinyl-only split single shared with the Fluid was to be

Nirvana's final Sub Pop release. Recorded live in February 1990 in Portland, Oregon, Cobain was supposedly against this Vaselines cover being released, feeling that the version was not as strong as it could have been. I'd tend to agree with him.

Overall rating ★

HERE SHE COMES NOW / VENUS IN FURS
(Split single with the Melvins, 1991)

Tracklisting: 'Here She Comes Now' / 'Venus in Furs' (by The Melvins)

Another vinyl-only split single, and another cover, this time of the Velvet Underground's 'Here She Comes Now'. A passable version which later appeared on With The Lights Out as well as a Velvet Underground tribute album, release was limited to only 1000 pressings in eight different colours.

Overall rating ★ ★

SMELLS LIKE TEEN SPIRIT
(Single, September 10, 1991)

Tracklisting: 'Smells Like Teen Spirit' / 'Drain You' / 'Even in His Youth' / 'Aneurysm'

This was the track that single-handedly launched Nirvana - and grunge - into the mainstream and started the 1990s alternative culture, giving the Generation X'ers an anthem to call their own. Not expected to be as big a hit as it was, 'Smells Like Teen Spirit' was intended to be the foundations of Nirvana, while the subsequent single, 'Come As You Are', was pencilled in as the main event. However, campus radio and modern rock radio stations picked it up and the rest is history. The classic music video didn't do it any harm either. A cultural event.

Overall rating ★ ★ ★ ★ ★

NEVERMIND
(Album, September 24, 1991)

Tracklisting: 'Smells Like Teen Spirit' / 'In Bloom' / 'Come As You Are' / 'Breed' / 'Lithium' / 'Polly' / 'Territorial Pissings' / 'Drain You' / 'Lounge Act' / 'Stay Away' / 'On a Plain' / 'Something in the Way' / 'Endless, Nameless' (hidden track)

Smells Like Teen Spirit ★ ★ ★ ★
Containing one of the most memorable riffs in music, 'Smells Like Teen Spirit' kicks off Nevermind in a very different vein to Bleach. Poppy and melodic, the track is a celebration of Cobain's pop-song-writing credibility. The opening chords of the track are sure to immortalise the band forever, in spite of being more than a little reminiscent of Boston's 1976 hit 'More Than a Feeling'. The introduction of Dave Grohl to the line-up, replacing Chad Channing on drums, makes an immediate impact - the way he crashes in with an athletic drum line is nothing short of thrilling. Cobain's nigh-on impossible-to-understand vocals reflect the tortured soul within that helped to launch the band into superstardom and connect to thousands of teenagers all across the globe.

In Bloom ★ ★ ★
One of the most confusingly ironic songs of all time, live Nirvana concerts found fans singing the lyrics back at the band in spite of their content: "He's the one / Who likes all our pretty songs / And he likes to sing along / And he likes to shoot his

gun / But he knows not what it means." Still, interesting chord changes, an anthemic chorus, a deep and catchy bass, and a great video (both of them) make this stand out as another great anthem for the masses and continued Nirvana's venture into the less grungey world of pop-rock.

Come As You Are ★ ★ ★

The third track, and the second single from Nevermind, opens with Kurt's instantly memorable, hooky riff. A wonderfully melodic vocal arrangement is accompanied by a haunting arrangement in this down-tempo number. The distinctive riff once again found Nirvana being accused of plagiarism, this time by British post-punkers Killing Joke. However, no lawsuit was filed, as apparently Nirvana freely admitted to Killing Joke frontman Jaz Coleman that they had indeed stolen the riff. Cobain's lyrics show much progress from Bleach, and refer to a drugs campaign in San Francisco in the 1980s "Come doused in mud, soaked in bleach." Cobain, of course, was a recognised user of heroin.

Breed ★ ★

Originally titled 'Immodium', but changed due to copyright issues, 'Breed' is a song written about Cobain's and Tad Doyle's (lead vocalist and guitarist of the band Tad) poor diets and road fatigue, which had led to sickness and diarrhoea. The vocals come in short, swift strokes, and the lyrics use repetition to maximum effect. Reminiscent of Bleach, this harks back to Nirvana's grungier beginnings, full of angst and punk riffs. The balance isn't quite right, and although Krist's bassline is chunky it is too loud for the guitar part, which has a powerful mega-distorted drive, but needs to be emphasised a whole lot more.

Lithium ★ ★ ★

A classic Nirvana song full of quotable lyrics: "I'm so happy / Cause today I found my friends / they're in my head" - and drug-related undertones. The song's title is often attributed to lithium's tendency to be found in mood-stabilising drugs, although again, in classic Nirvana style, there has been much debate about the actual meaning of the song. Simple and effective, but with unusually complex bass runs by Krist, 'Lithium' marks itself out as a solid grunge anthem on an album full of pop-rock songs. A really juicy song, with interesting drums from Grohl, 'Lithium' is let down by over-production in the studio taking something away from a track that works better live.

Polly ★ ★ ★ ★

Based on the true story of a girl who was abducted while returning from a punk-rock show, and consequently raped and tortured, 'Polly' dates back to at least 1989 and stands as one of Cobain's earliest experiments into pop songwriting. It was omitted from Bleach, as Cobain thought it was too inconsistent with the band's heavy grunge sound of the time. An acoustic guitar is also used to good effect for the first time in Nirvana's studio albums, and a four-note lyric style is reflected throughout, adding to the potent simplicity of the track.

Territorial Pissings ★ ★ ★ ★

A sneaky peak into Nirvana's punk origins, 'Territorial Pissings' is believed to be about Cobain's childhood fantasies of being an alien, containing, as it does, the lyrics, "Just because you're paranoid / don't mean they're not after you", a variation of a quote by conspiracist Robert Anton Wilson. An undoubted favourite of many avid Nirvana fans, the beat on 'Territorial Pissings' comes in loud and hard, and just 16 seconds into the song the exiting drums really drive in. Kurt's raw vocals are displayed right until the last in this all-punk, two-and-a-half minute classic.

Drain You ★ ★ ★ ★

A personal favourite of Cobain's, he once said he wished 'Drain

You' was as famous as 'Smells Like Teen Spirit', as he loved playing it live. Written about his relationship with Bikini Kill's Tobi Vail, much to Courtney Love's constant disdain, 'Drain You' contains more guitar overdubs than any other song on the album -six- and sounds completely different live than it does on record. The strange noises in the middle section are made by children's toys Cobain brought into the studio.

Lounge Act ★ ★

"Truth - covered in security / I can't let you smother me" are the lyrics that kick off this rather twee song, again written about Vail. The title comes from the band feeling that the song sounded like a lounge song that a bar band would play. It does, and that's not a particularly good thing. One of the weaker tracks on the album, it still has a great bassline and picks up when Cobain sings up an octave at the end of the track, making this nothing more than an average offering.

Stay Away ★ ★

Despite some more fairly solid lyric work from Cobain, 'Stay Away' joins 'Lounge Act' as another mediocre song, although like 'Lounge Act', and to some extent 'Drain You', it manages to keep Bleach fans happy with its punk sensibilities. The line Cobain screams at the end of the song, "God is gay", comes from graffiti he supposedly used to spray paint on buildings as a youngster. Originally entitled 'Pay to Play', 'Stay Away' sounds like a take on a Nirvana song rather than one of their best.

On a Plain ★ ★ ★

Supposedly about either alienation or nothing at all, depending on who you listen to, 'On a Plain' is a well-rounded song with another good Novoselic bassline that holds together well. Yet another fine pop song on their first mainstream album, the influence of the Beatles and Bob Dylan on Cobain's songwriting shines most brightly here.

Something in the Way ★ ★ ★ ★ ★

An ending, of sorts, (see Endless, Nameless) to Nevermind, and a wonderful ending at that, making this an essential Nirvana track and one of their best. Haunting, dark, and lyrically fantastic: "It's okay to eat fish / 'Cause they don't have any feelings", 'Something in the Way' contains another first for Nirvana with the use of a cello on the track. Thanks to a combination of the relatively slow timing of the song, the song's gentle mood, and Cobain's strangely tuned guitar, Novoselic, Grohl, and Kirk Canning (the cellist) all had difficulties adding their parts to it, but this barely evident during this superb closing track on a seminal album.

Endless, Nameless (hidden track) ★

Containing distorted, loud vocals and siren-like guitars, hidden track 'Endless Nameless' bares no relevance to the rest of the album as a whole. This is wild, messy, and very heavy, utilising thick distortion and anti-guitar solos, making it more of a jam session than a proper track. A mystery as to how it made it to the final cut.

Conclusion

Nevermind's sound is so familiar, even to this day, because of the influence it has had on thousands of rock records which tried to capture its energy and melodic sensibility, mostly without success. Few albums have occupied our cultural consciousness like this one, and many of the songs still stand up today as being classics. The record's historical weight can make it hard to hear now with fresh ears, and perhaps it isn't quite the record most people make it out to be, but the musical significance and Cobain's lyrical urgency make this stand out as a classic breakthrough album for alternative rock.

Overall rating ★ ★ ★

COME AS YOU ARE
(Single, March 3, 1992)

Tracklisting: 'Come as You Are' / 'Endless, Nameless' / 'School' (live from Seattle, Washington, 1991) / 'Drain You' (live from Seattle, 1991)

A great song and, after 'Smells Like Teen Spirit', Nevermind's second most successful single. Much was made of the lyric, "And I swear that I don't have a gun" after Cobain's death, though the song was written over three years earlier. Still, that's the media for you. This also includes a couple of energetic live performances.

Overall rating ★ ★ ★

HORMOANING
(EP, February 5, 1992)

Tracklisting: 'Turnaround' / 'Aneurysm' / 'D-7' / 'Son of a Gun' / 'Even in His Youth' / 'Molly's Lips'

Released primarily in Australia and labelled as a Tour EP, on original release this five-track EP included a couple of rarities. However, by the end of the year and the release of Incesticide, that had become a thing of the past. Still, four covers and two original Nirvana tracks make this EP a nonetheless solid affair. Also released in Japan, Hormoaning is only for completists.

Overall rating ★ ★

LITHIUM
(Single, July 21, 1992)

Tracklisting: 'Lithium' / 'Been A Son' (live from Seattle, 1991) / 'Curmudgeon'

Ranked highly by numerous magazine surveys and covered by the likes of Papa Roach and the Polyphonic Spree, 'Lithium' was the third of four singles released from Nirvana's breakthrough album. A classic live performance of 'Been A Son', and 'Curmudgeon', which eventually made it onto the 2004 box set, With the Lights Out, complete this nice little package.

Overall rating ★ ★ ★

IN BLOOM
(Single, Novemeber 30, 1992)

Tracklisting: 'In Bloom' / 'Sliver' (live from Del Mar, California, 1991) / 'Polly' (live from Del Mar, 1991)

It's no surprise that Nevermind's singles' B-sides were so packed full of live performances, as this encompassed the hysteria surrounding Nirvana at the time. 'In Bloom' is a great song in its own right, and comes into its own here.

Overall rating ★ ★ ★

NEVERMIND: IT'S AN INTERVIEW
(Interview CD, 1992)

An excellent insight into Nirvana at the peak of their success, this interview by Boston radio station WFNX contains over an hour of audio interview with live and studio recordings. Most songs on the CD are incomplete, but there are a few full live versions, including 'About A Girl', 'On a Plain', and the same live versions of 'Drain You' and 'School' that can be found on the 'Come As You Are' single released a few months previously. Worth taking in.

Overall rating ★ ★ ★

INCESTICIDE
(Compilation Album, December 14, 1992)

Tracklisting: 'Dive' / 'Sliver' / 'Stain' / 'Been a Son' / 'Turnaround' / 'Molly's Lips' / 'Son of a Gun' / '(New Wave) Polly' / 'Beeswax' / 'Downer' / 'Mexican Seafood' / 'Hairspray Queen' / 'Aero Zeppelin' / 'Big Long Now' / 'Aneurysm'

Dive ★ ★
Both 'Dive' and 'Sliver' make up one of the band's earliest seven-inch singles and kick things off nicely. A heavy, mid-paced opener, 'Dive' starts Incesticide in relatively fine style and is, for those interested in these things, Courtney Love's favourite Nirvana song. Cobain himself was less sure dismissing it as, "yet another rewrite of the heavy string-bend grunge formula."

Sliver ★ ★ ★
Assumed to be about an incident from Cobain's childhood, and the second half of the classic early seven-inch single, 'Sliver' is the poppier of the two, and probably the second-best track on this B-sides and rarities album. Great lyrics and use of repetition here make it no surprise that this found its way onto the Best of… album in 2002.

Stain ★
A very similar track in scope and style to 'Dive', but not as good. A heavy, mid-paced rocker and nothing more….

Been a Son ★ ★

Similar to 'Stain' in more ways than one, it seems a little odd that the two are paired together here. Then again, the covers are all next to each other, as are the seven-inch single tracks, so why not these as well? Still, in spite of similar riffs, 'Been a Son' is the stronger of the two tracks, and also made it onto the Best Of ... album alongside 'Sliver'. Released in at least six different versions over the years, this version finds Krist falling out of love with the inelegant, chunky bass solo, which could be the reason why the track was later re-recorded with a guitar solo instead.

Turnaround ★ ★

The first of three covers on the album is a version of Devo's 'Turnaround'. The lyrics may not have been written by Cobain, but he certainly puts his own twist on them and makes them as his own. "Take a step outside the planet / Turn around and around / Take a look at where you are / It's pretty scary." A nice take on a great song.

Molly's Lips ★ ★ ★

The first of the two Vaselines covers on Incesticide, 'Molly's Lips' had always been a staple live track for Cobain and Co. With a sound not dissimilar to the one to be found on Nevermind, the track has an upbeat guitar sound and is a definite step away from Cobain's usual lyrical style.

Son of a Gun ★ ★

Another Vaselines cover, and another catchy one at that. Similar guitar riffs to 'Molly's Lips' come as no real surprise, but the track stands up pretty well regardless. "The sun shines in the bedroom / When we play / The raining always starts / When you go away."

(New Wave) Polly ★ ★

A fresh take on one of the band's better-known classics from Nevermind, '(New Wave) Polly', recorded as an electric studio version for a BBC Evening Session in late 1991, is more up-tempo than Nevermind's acoustic version, and, to be brutally honest, sounds like nothing more than a pretty average cover version of a great track.

Beeswax ★

From here on out we have what could be dubbed the meat of the record, as the songs become more twisting, experimental, and musically interesting. 'Beeswax' utilises a heavy-guitar, grunge-based sound, and after hearing it it's no surprise to find out that it was recorded back in Nirvana's early days in 1988. References to the medical use of beeswax for painkilling come alongside other, frankly, curious lyrics: "Push the assbutton / Tweeking and flexing if the wind blows just right / Tacky and thumbs on polyester / Highwater jumpsuits and a raped ape." Hmmm …

Downer ★ ★

Also featured on Bleach, 'Downer' was written by Cobain for his previous band, Fecal Matter.

Mexican Seafood ★

This version of 'Mexican Seafood' was, again, recorded way back when, and features Dale Crover of the Melvins hard-hitting on drums. The song appears to be about a yeast infection. Should've been left well alone.

Hairspray Queen ★ ★

Not great, but not a disaster - lyrically poor, but musically passable. "I was you mine, you were mine, my enemy / You were, mine, I was your, your enemy."

Aero Zeppelin ★ ★ ★

Recorded in 1988, 'Aero Zeppelin' is more of a rock and roll parody than a stereotypical Nirvana track. "All the kids will eat it up if it's packaged properly." Still, it holds up well and comes as one of the brighter spots on the album. Unique in comparison to other Nirvana tracks due to its light opening, the main riff has an oriental sound, although it gains some aggression as the song progresses. The lyrics are, without doubt, an attack launched on conformity and mainstream '80s pop culture, with topics including songwriting, fashion, and fan devotion. The title - obviously - combines the names of so-called classic rock bands Aerosmith and Led Zeppelin.

Big Long Now ★ ★ ★

Long, slow, and a similar sound to the one which Alice in Chains employed a few years after it was recorded. It has an eerie quality which makes for an interesting sound far removed from the band's usual fare.

Aneurysm ★ ★ ★ ★

'Aneurysm' is the best track to be found on this B-sides album, and a great way to end the record. Heavy, grungey, and in a different key to the version to be found on the 'Smells Like Teen Spirit' single, 'Aneurysm' was inspired by Cobain's break-up with a girlfriend at the time of writing - Tobi Vail, of course. A BBC Radio 1 poll taken in 2000 actually saw it voted as the third best Nirvana song by listeners, toppled only by 'Smells Like Teen Spirit' and 'Heart-Shaped Box'.

Conclusion

It seems to most of those on the outside that Incesticide was nothing more than a gap-filler, a means of gathering B-sides and other bits and bobs that Nirvana had lying around in the archives before the next full studio album came along. The result is a lightweight affair, even if some of the content is pretty good. Cobain's liner notes are particularly harrowing, however, sounding eerily like his suicide note, deriding the fame and money that ultimately wiped him out. Uneven, but not without its charm.

Overall rating ★ ★

OH, THE GUILT / PUSS
(Split single with the Jesus Lizard, 1992)

Tracklisting: 'Oh, the Guilt' / 'Puss' (by the Jesus Lizard)

Yet another split single, this time with fellow American rockers the Jesus Lizard. 'Oh, the Guilt' was actually Nirvana's first release after Nevermind, and is a great track – straight, bloody, uncompromising rock, well worth a listen. It's also featured on the 2004 box set, With the Lights Out.

Overall rating ★ ★ ★

HEART-SHAPED BOX
(Single, August 1993)

Tracklisting: 'Heart-Shaped Box' / 'Milk It' / 'Marigold'

In many ways this track is the epitome of the album that followed it: it is Cobain's and 'Heart-Shaped Box's' fascination with the female body that provides the underlying theme of In Utero. Ranked highly in almost every music magazines' all-time-great lists, 'Heart-Shaped Box' proved to be a huge commercial and musical success for Nirvana and stands up well today. The single also includes an interesting song, 'Marigold', penned by future Foo Fighters frontman and Nirvana sticksman Dave Grohl.

Overall rating ★ ★ ★ ★

IN UTERO

(Album, September 21, 1993)

Tracklisting: 'Serve the Servants' / 'Scentless Apprentice' / 'Heart-Shaped Box' / 'Rape Me' / 'Frances Farmer Will Have Her Revenge On Seattle' / 'Dumb' / 'Very Ape' / 'Milk It' / 'Pennyroyal Tea' / 'Radio Friendly Unit Shifter' / 'Tourette's' / 'All Apologies' / 'Gallons Of Rubbing Alcohol Flow Through The Strip' (jam recorded in Rio de Janeiro)

Serve the Servants ★ ★ ★

An excellent open track to In Utero, 'Serve the Servants' has a great melody and a stately chorus which allows the understated verses to shine. Noticeably more raw and less slick than Nevermind, Grohl's hard-hitting style fits in well with the lyrics here, which address a number of issues, including the negative media surrounding Courtney Love: "If she floats then she is not / A witch, like we had thought", and also the band's fame and Cobain's apathy concerning their mainstream exposure in the very opening couplet: "Teenage angst has paid off well / Now I'm bored and old." 'Serve the Servants' boded well for the rest of the album, although it eventually pales in comparison with much of what follows.

Scentless Apprentice ★ ★ ★

Intense fuzzy production laid over a commanding guitar riff and menacing, yet amusing, lyrics really show how far removed In Utero was from Nevermind. After being introduced to the album via 'Serve the Servants', we are treated to a track which bares strong resemblance to the Bleach era, full of energy and malice. Based on one of Cobain's all-time favourite novels, Perfume, by Patrick Süskind, 'Scentless Apprentice' is strange in that it is listed as one of the few Nirvana songs to which all three members of the band contributed. The song's main guitar riff was actually written by Grohl and shows a good grounding for the heady heights at which he would find himself a few years later with Foo Fighters.

Heart-Shaped Box ★ ★ ★ ★

Despite all of its graphic imagery ("Meat-eating orchids forgive no one just yet"), it came as no surprise that 'Heart-Shaped Box' was released as the first single from the album. As the album's one major hit, 'Heart-shaped Box' stands up both as a great single and as one that slots in well with the feel of the album as a whole. A dark rock ballad, the guitar solo and Novoselic's growling bass are completely distinct from past Nirvana work. According to Love, the song was written in less than five minutes in a giant closet. Whatever works for you, I guess.

Rape Me ★ ★ ★

A riff purposefully manipulated and mangled from 'Smells Like Teen Spirit' and coupled with lyrics that have no commercial appeal at all ("Hate me / Do it and do it again / Waste me / Rape me, my friend"), 'Rape Me' finds Cobain in typical anarchic form. As a statement of intent, the album's second single (double A-side with 'All Apologies') is excellent, and it's not bad musically, either. Its swirling bridge is certainly a highlight, and Grohl's hard, energetic drumming makes the track difficult to dislike. Cobain insisted in interviews that 'Rape Me' is an anti-rape song, in which a man rapes a woman, gets sent to prison, and ends up being raped there himself. It is seen by many as the sequel to 'Polly'.

Frances Farmer Will Have Her Revenge On Seattle ★ ★ ★ ★

Another outstanding track in the same vein as album opener 'Serve the Servants'. A great chorus and more Cobain gold ("I miss the comfort in being sad") make sure the album continues strongly. Another raw song in the Bleach mould, 'Frances Farmer ...' keeps the well-used Nirvana quiet/loud formula. It refers to Seattle-born actress Frances Farmer who, amongst other things, was accused of being an atheist, was declared legally insane because of her paranoid schizophrenia, and battled with manic depression in the mid 1940s. Cobain - not surprisingly - felt a certain kinship with her.

Dumb ★ ★ ★ ★

Often cited as being In Utero's 'Polly', 'Dumb' has obvious similarities with Nevermind's tale of rape and abduction, but has a more delicate sound and a small string section, something which Nirvana began to favour as the years went by and their career came to an abrupt end. A sweet drum pattern by Grohl, combined with an aching cello part, create a slow, steady, and melodic track. It has been said that 'Dumb' was inspired by Cobain's envy for people who are seemingly able to move through life without ever feeling sad or depressed.

Very Ape ★ ★ ★

The hard-rocking 'Very Ape' is the most obvious nod to Bleach on the album. Utilising a style not dissimilar to that to be found on 'Blew', 'Very Ape' has a catchy riff and some great quick, small, drum rolls by Grohl. The lyrics address Cobain's age-old bugbear of machismo, evident in many of the band's other songs, most notably 'Territorial Pissings'.

Milk It ★ ★ ★

Probably the most rabid, vicious song Cobain wrote for any of the band's three studio albums, 'Milk It' has a murky, free-wheeling sound, which Cobain attributed as being the sound of the "new Nirvana". The lyrics continue the obsession with human anatomy and the female form ("I own my own pet virus / I get to pet and name her / Her milk is my shit / My shit is her milk"), and also allude to Cobain's eventual demise ("Look on the bright side is suicide"). Again, Nirvana utilises the quiet/ loud formula here, with the quiet verses loaded with menace almost fooling you into thinking that they are the sections with bite and malice. The chorus is snarling and memorable: "Doll steak! Test meat!"

Pennyroyal Tea ★ ★ ★

Widely, and unfairly, derided by fans because Courtney Love supposedly played a large part in the songwriting process, 'Pennyroyal Tea' isn't actually that bad. OK it's hardly a classic and the MTV Unplugged version certainly stands out as being the more essential track, showing that sometimes more can be achieved by taking a less heavy approach. Forlorn lyrics over a travelling guitar solo are a splendid representation of what Cobain's life had become: "I'm so tired I can't sleep / I'm anaemic royalty."

Radio Friendly Unit Shifter ★ ★

"I was just wondering … do you like me?", whispered at the beginning of the track, and another display of Cobain's confusion about the band's spiralling success, 'Radio Friendly Unit Shifter' is a hard-edged, chaotic mess and - along with 'Tourette's' - is probably the least important track on the album. Cobain and Novoselic's stop-and-go motion, coupled with distortion, take this song to new and different levels. Grohl's performance is, for once, rather outshone by his band mates.

Tourette's ★ ★

'Tourette's' is dominated by Cobain's vocal warblings, and was actually conceived long before the album came out. The band revised the structure and tacked it on to the end of the album as nothing more than filler. They rarely played 'Tourette's' in concert, as Cobain considered it to be a meaningless throwaway song. When they did perform it he sang it differently every time, and it shouldn't be considered anything more than a Pearl Jamesque jam session. It is musically cohesive, though, and to these ears is still worth a listen.

All Apologies ★ ★ ★ ★ ★

Undoubtedly Cobain's and Nirvana's most mature composition, it was actually a commercial flop as a single, an amazing injustice considering that this was a grunge song like no other. 'All Apologies' is a spiralling, beautiful piece ending with an intelligent coda, which finds Cobain singing, "All in all is all we are" over and over as the music fades away. Its infamous guitar riff, cello, and hollow lyrics make 'All Apologies' a fitting end to the band's final full studio release. A swan song of sorts, 'All Apologies' was actually written in 1990.

Gallons Of Rubbing Alcohol Flow Through The Strip ★

Just like the hidden track 'Endless, Nameless' from Nevermind, 'Gallons Of Rubbing Alcohol Flow Through The Strip' is pretty pointless. Not quite as bad as the noise fest of it's Nevermind counterpart, but still a poor song which bares no relevance to the well-rounded, perfectly realised album that came before it.

Conclusion

Nirvana's third and final studio album is also their best. More abrasive and less mainstream than Nevermind, but more polished and grown-up than Bleach, In Utero is the perfect mix of the two, and displays Nirvana's talent for producing both perfect pop and focused chaos, and making them work alongside each other in almost perfect harmony.

Overall rating ★ ★ ★ ★

ALL APOLOGIES / RAPE ME
(Double A-side Single, December 1993)

Tracklisting: 'All Apologies' / 'Rape Me' / 'Moist Vagina'

Possibly the best song Nirvana ever wrote, 'All Apologies' is matched up with the irony-tinged 'Rape Me' and lyrically obvious 'Moist Vagina', both of which had name changes to gain access to corporate stores such as Wal-Mart ('Waif Me' and 'MV', for what it's worth). Whether this was done so they wouldn't alienate fans (much like what Metallica did with 'Nothing Else Matters' in the early 90s, and Green Day did with 'Good Riddance [Time of Your Life]' in the late 90s) who knows, but there was no real need. At this point we all knew who Nirvana were.

Overall rating ★ ★ ★ ★ ★

PENNYROYAL TEA
(Single, April 1994)

Tracklisting: 'Pennyroyal Tea' / 'I Hate Myself and Want to Die' / 'Where Did You Sleep Last Night'

Released in the month of Cobain's untimely death, this single was soon scrapped and any copies that were released were soon recalled. Any copies that are kicking around are now - morbidly – collectors' items which go for big bucks. The single itself is a good one, containing two awesome B-sides: the rabid and prophetic 'I Hate Myself and Want to Die', and the classic Leadbelly folk song, 'Where Did You Sleep Last Night'.

Overall rating ★ ★ ★ ★

ABOUT A GIRL /
SOMETHING IN THE WAY
(Live, MTV Unplugged in New York, 1993)
(Single, October 24, 1994)

Released as Nirvana's MTV Unplugged in New York's only commercial single, this double A-side is undoubtedly good, but nothing more than a collector's piece.

Overall rating ★ ★ ★

NIRVANA:
MTV UNPLUGGED IN
NEW YORK
(Live Album, November 1, 1994)

Tracklisting: 'About a Girl' / 'Come as You Are' / 'Jesus Doesn't Want Me for a Sunbeam' / 'The Man Who Sold The World' / 'Pennyroyal Tea' / 'Dumb' / 'Polly' / 'On a Plain' / 'Something In The Way' / 'Plateau' / 'Oh, Me' / 'Lake of Fire' / 'All Apologies' / 'Where Did You Sleep Last Night'

About a Girl ★ ★ ★ ★ ★
Nirvana's first release after the death of Cobain begins with quiet applause before the band break into Bleach's 'About a Girl'. Guitars and understated drums are most audible in this, the most familiar reading of the track. Unlike the rest of the MTV Unplugged session, 'About a Girl' finds Cobain singing in his raspy, hard-edged voice.

Come as You Are ★ ★ ★ ★
Unlike the rest of the album, 'Come as You Are' - taken, of course, from Nevermind - stands up as the only track that remains similar to its parent version, both in structure and

sound. Emotional and pleading, Cobain's voice here is the key element to its success.

Jesus Doesn't Want Me for a Sunbeam ★ ★ ★ ★ ★

The first of the album's numerous covers, the Vaselines' 'Jesus Doesn't Want Me for a Sunbeam' (actually incorrectly titled from the original 'Jesus Don't Want Me For a Sunbeam') is one of the finest songs on the album. Touching and musically diverse, Novoselic makes his appearance on the track with an accordion in hand. Cobain manages to bare his soul with a track that isn't his own; with this performance, he manages to make it so.

The Man Who Sold the World ★ ★ ★ ★

A cover of David Bowie's early 70s song, 'The Man Who Sold the World' utilises guest cellist Lori Goldston to good effect, providing a haunting melody to the track's stirring lyrics: "Oh no, not me / we never lost control / you're face to face / With The Man Who Sold The World."

Pennyroyal Tea ★ ★ ★ ★

Only Cobain and his pawn-shop-bought guitar feature on this one, in a pure, emotionally wrought performance. One of the better examples out there of the true power of both Cobain's voice and lyrical talents, 'Pennyroyal Tea' has an excellent use of dynamics, as Kurt moves from his quiet, raspy singing voice in the verses to a more powerful chorus.

Dumb ★ ★ ★ ★

A straightforward reading of one of the band's lesser-appreciated classics, haunting vocals from Cobain once more fit the lyrical content perfectly here: "I'm not like them / but I can pretend." More superb cello playing from Goldston adds to the effect.

Polly ★ ★ ★ ★

Yet another version of 'Polly', the third in only five albums, and it's a fine version at that. Cobain and his guitar, Pat Smear on rhythm guitar, and an accompanying cello in the background are all this track needs to send out its raw emotion. Cobain was reluctant to play 'Polly' directly after 'Dumb', musing that they were "exactly the same song."

On a Plain ★ ★ ★ ★

Taken from Nevermind, this terrific version of 'On a Plain' sees the whole band rejoin the session: "The finest day that I've ever had / was when I learned to cry on command."

Something in The Way ★ ★ ★ ★ ★

Again featuring Smear on rhythm guitar and Goldston on cello 'Something in the Way' plods along as Cobain sings in his dark, pensive way, in a particularly chilling, and exceptional, reading of the song.

Plateau ★ ★ ★ ★

'Plateau' is the first of three Meat Puppets covers on the disk, with Cobain employing his cynical, spitting vocals. The Kirkwood brothers themselves appear on all three tracks.

Oh, Me ★ ★ ★ ★

As in 'Plateau', 'Oh, Me' is a powerful rendition of another Meat Puppets classic. Superb vocals complement the quiet instrumentation perfectly.

Lake of Fire ★ ★ ★ ★ ★

"Where do bad folks go when they die / they don't go to heaven where the angels fly / Go to a lake of fire and fry / don't see them again 'til the Fourth of July." This is haunting and memorable stuff; Cobain makes these terrific lyrics his own with a powerful vocal performance.

All Apologies ★ ★ ★ ★ ★

As on its parent album, 'All Apologies' could well have been a fitting end to the album, but, alas, it wasn't to be, as 'Where Did You Sleep Last Night' grabbed those particular honours. A simple but emotional reading of the song, it stays quite close to the original acoustic rendering, but somehow feels more personal. The additional cello from Goldston certainly doesn't hinder the performance.

Where Did You Sleep Last Night ★ ★ ★ ★ ★

"My girl, my girl, don't lie to me / Tell me where did you sleep last night?" 'Where Did You Sleep Last Night' closes the album almost perfectly. On this dark haunting cover of an old classic folk song, the singer's passion and pain sum up exactly what Cobain and Nirvana were all about. It illustrates with crushing clarity what lay behind their mainstream and musical appeal and provided an exceptional end to an exceptional album.

Conclusion

Recorded shortly before Cobain's demise, MTV Unplugged's, pared down, sparse recordings of some of their most commercially successful and popular tracks have lost none of their potency and are a testament to the band's ability to transcend the grunge sound with which they were so commonly associated. This timeless collection is an insight into a tortured mind and soul, as Cobain opens himself up to the world, no longer hiding behind a wall of sound, but instead presenting pop classics with a rich, full, emotive sound unmatched by anything else in the Nirvana back catalogue. It comes as no surprise that the album won a Grammy for Best Alternative Music Album in 1996. Immutable.

Overall rating ★ ★ ★ ★ ★

LIVE! TONIGHT! SOLD OUT!!
(VHS, 1994, reissued on DVD, 2006)

A fine collection of live performances compiled by Cobain but unfinished at the time of his death. Novoselic, Grohl, and director Kevin Kerslake teamed up to complete this stockpile of live footage mostly recorded during the Nevermind period and it's well worth investigating.

Overall rating ★ ★ ★ ★

THE MAN WHO SOLD THE WORLD
(Live, MTV Unplugged in New York, 1993)
(Promotional Single, 1994)

Tracklisting: The Man Who Sold the World

Promotional single for radio playlists. Nothing more.

Overall rating ★ ★

WHERE DID YOU SLEEP LAST NIGHT
(Live, MTV Unplugged in New York, 1993)
(Promotional Single, 1995)

Tracklisting: 'Where Did You Sleep Last Night'

See 'The Man Who Sold the World' above – a great track, but non-essential.

Overall rating ★ ★

SINGLES
(Singles Box Set, December 1995)

Includes the singles: 'Smells Like Teen Spirit' / 'Come as You Are' / 'In Bloom' / 'Lithium' / 'Heart-Shaped Box' / 'All Apologies'

A box set comprised of the singles from Nirvana's two biggest studio albums, Nevermind and In Utero. At this point everything was available on other major releases, aside from the demo of 'Aneurysm', which, although it appeared on the 'Smells Like Teen Spirit' single, was difficult to track down. Eventually even this was released in the 2004 box set With the Lights Out.

Overall rating ★ ★

ANEURYSM
(Live, Del Mar, CA, 1991, Promotional Single, 1996)

Tracklisting: 'Aneurysm'

A promotional single for the upcoming release of the live album From the Muddy Banks of the Wishkah.

Overall rating ★ ★

DRAIN YOU
(Live, Del Mar, CA, 1991, Promotional Single, 1996)

Tracklisting: 'Drain You'

Another promo single released and intended for radio play in the U.S., from the compiled live album From the Muddy Banks of the Wishkah.

Overall rating ★ ★

FROM THE MUDDY BANKS OF THE WISHKAH

(Live Album, October 1, 1996)

Tracklisting: 'Intro' (from London, 1989) / 'School' (from Amsterdam, 1991) / 'Drain You' (from Del Mar, California, 1991) / 'Aneurysm' (from Del Mar, 1991) / 'Smells Like Teen Spirit' (from Del Mar, 1991) / 'Been a Son' (from Amsterdam, 1991) / 'Lithium' (from Amsterdam, 1991) / 'Sliver' (from Springfield, Massachusetts, 1993) / 'Spank Thru' (from Rome, 1991) / 'Scentless Apprentice' (from Seattle, 1993) / 'Heart-Shaped Box' (from Inglewood, California, 1993) / 'Milk It' (from Seattle, 1994) / 'Negative Creep' (from Seattle, 1991) / 'Polly' (from London, 1991) / 'Breed' (from London, 1989) / 'Tourette's' (from Reading Festival, 1992) / 'Blew' (from Amsterdam, 1991) / concert out-takes (from various)

Conclusion

The second in a long, long line of posthumous Nirvana albums, From the Muddy Banks of the Wishkah came a full two years after MTV Unplugged was released. Compiled by Novoselic and Grohl, the album is an energetic, loud, frenzied one, in complete contrast to MTV Unplugged in New York. It almost feels as if Grohl and Novoselic had an agenda in putting this album together because up until this point MTV Unplugged was being played non-stop on MTV and was largely perceived as music for a wake. That acoustic detour aside, Nirvana live was full of life, energy, and vigour and From the Muddy Banks of the Wishkah offers the proof, with 16 tracks spanning the length and breadth of the band's career. All sixteen tracks are seemingly the sloppiest versions available! 'Lithium', 'Aneurysm' and 'Breed' overflow with intensity, and 'Smells

Like Teen Spirit' has never sounded better. This album is a true testament to Nirvana's status as a premier live band, and one that is still sorely missed.

Overall rating ★ ★ ★ ★

YOU KNOW YOU'RE RIGHT
(Promotional Single, October 8, 2002)

Tracklisting: 'You Know You're Right'

Tinged with controversy, 'You Know You're Right' was released as a promotional single, but thanks to Internet sales actually managed to chart in the U.S. One of the few post-In Utero Nirvana compositions known to exist, 'You Know You're Right' is a collector's piece of sorts, and a good track at that. For years, it was known only from a bootlegged live version from late 1993, and also from a MTV Unplugged set by Hole in 1995. It was eventually released on the Best Of … record.

Overall rating ★ ★ ★ ★

NIRVANA
(Compilation Album, October 29, 2002)

Tracklisting: 'You Know You're Right' / 'About a Girl' / 'Been a Son' / 'Sliver' / 'Smells Like Teen Spirit' / 'Come as You Are' / 'Lithium' / 'In Bloom' / 'Heart-Shaped Box' / 'Pennyroyal Tea' (Scott Litt remix) / 'Rape Me' / 'Dumb' / 'All Apologies' (Unplugged in New York, 1993) / 'The Man Who Sold the World' (Unplugged in New York, 1993)

You Know You're Right ★ ★ ★ ★

The only previously unreleased track on the album, 'You Know You're Right' starts with the gentle sound of guitar strings being strummed, setting the tone for this song of manic depression. Significant grunge grooves from Cobain and Novoselic, and a sturdy Grohl drum pattern are shared by Cobain's famed wail and classic lyrical prowess: "Whistle and I'll come outside / I no longer have to hide / Let's talk about someone else she just wants to love herself / She just moves away from here she just wants to love herself / And I won't move away from here you won't be afraid of fear / I am walking in the piss always knew it'd come to this / I have never felt so well things have never been so well." Cobain then elevates the tension as he screeches "pain" in a long, drawn-out cry for help, accompanied by a seething guitar riff. It was a fine addition to the Nirvana catalogue.

Conclusion

The third Nirvana album to be released following Cobain's death in April 1994 and the first to feature studio material, Nirvana is a best-of compilation featuring all of the band's most popular offerings. It has a selection from Nevermind, a selection from In Utero, a selection from the pre-Nevermind era, and a couple of tracks from MTV Unplugged in New York. This record is Nirvana the rock band, Nirvana the stars of MTV - diet Nirvana if you will. There is no real anger here, no passion, no 'Territorial Pissings', or 'Scentless Apprentice'. Aside from 'You Know You're Right' (which pushes this atrocity up a star all by itself), this is nothing more than a money making exercise.

Overall rating ★ ★

WITH THE LIGHTS OUT
(Box Set, November 23, 2004)

Disc 1 Tracklisting: 'Heartbreaker' (live from Raymond, Washington, 1987) / 'Anorexorcist' / 'White Lace and Strange' / 'Help Me, I'm Hungry' (all from KAOS radio show, 1987) / 'Mrs. Butterworth' (demo, 1987) / 'If You Must' / 'Pen Cap Chew' (both from a studio session in Seattle, 1988) / 'Downer' / 'Floyd the Barber' / 'Raunchola' / 'Moby Dick' (all live from Tacoma, Washington, 1988) / 'Beans' / 'Don't Want It All' / 'Clean Up Before She Comes' / 'Polly' / 'About a Girl' (home recordings, 1987 & 1988) / 'Blandest' (studio session from Seattle, 1988) / 'Dive' (studio session from Olympia, Washington, 1989) / 'They Hung Him on a Cross' / 'Grey Goose' / 'Ain't It a Shame' (all from a studio session for the Jury, a Leadbelly cover band, from Seattle, 1989) / 'Token Eastern Song' / 'Even in His Youth' / 'Polly' (all from a studio session from Seattle, 1989)

Disc 1 details the band's exploits in and around the release of Bleach, when Cobain and Co. were desperately trying to find a unique voice, a good drummer, and a way out of Aberdeen, Washington. A couple of Led Zeppelin covers, three classic Leadbelly tracks recorded way back in 1989, and live versions of some of the best moments from Bleach, including 'Floyd the Barber' and 'Downer', are some of the highlights here. In truth, Disc 1 merely illustrates the foundations that were being built for the future Nirvana sound but it's a worthwhile collection nonetheless.

Overall rating ★ ★

Disc 2 Tracklisting: 'Opinion' / 'Lithium' / 'Been a Son' (all from an acoustic performance from KAOS radio show, 1990) / 'Sliver' / 'Where Did You Sleep Last Night' (both from demos, 1990) / 'Pay to Play' / 'Here She Comes Now' (both from a studio session from Madison, Wisconsin, 1990) / 'Drain You' (demo, 1991) / 'Aneurysm' (studio session from Seattle, 1991) / 'Smells Like Teen Spirit' (demo, 1991) / 'Breed' / 'Verse Chorus Verse' / 'Old Age' (all from a studio session from Van Nuys, California, 1991) / 'Endless, Nameless' / 'Dumb' (both from a John Peel radio session, 1991) / 'D-7' (from a John Peel radio session, 1990) / 'Oh, the Guilt' / 'Curmudgeon' / 'Return of the Rat' (all from a studio session from Seattle, 1992) / 'Smells Like Teen Spirit' (from the Nevermind studio session from Van Nuys, 1991)

The second disc features various mixes and live performances from the Nevermind era, which saw Nirvana propelled to the dizzying heights that we still remember. An early 'Smells Like Teen Spirit', plus solid alternative versions of 'Pay to Play' (Stay Away), 'Lithium', and 'Breed'. It's all a bit polished, but a few radio sessions (particularly the John Peel sessions) make sections of Disc 2 well worth a listen.

Overall rating ★ ★

Disc 3 Tracklisting: 'Rape Me' (demo, 1991) / 'Rape Me' (studio session from Seattle, 1992) / 'Scentless Apprentice' (demo, 1992) / 'Heart-Shaped Box' / 'I Hate Myself and Want to Die' / 'Milk It' / 'Moist Vagina' / 'Gallons of Rubbing Alcohol Flow Through The Strip' / 'The Other Improv' (all from a studio session in Rio de Janeiro, Brazil, 1993) / 'Serve the Servants' /

'Very Ape' (both from a demo, 1992) / 'Pennyroyal Tea' (demo, 1993) / 'Marigold' / 'Sappy' (both from the In Utero studio session from Cannon Falls, Michigan, 1993) / 'Jesus Doesn't Want Me for a Sunbeam' (demo, 1994) / 'Do Re Mi' (demo, 1994) / 'You Know You're Right' (demo, 1993 or 1994) / 'All Apologies' (demo, 1991 or 1992)

The best disc of the box set, CD 3 opens with two different versions of 'Rape Me'; the first acoustic, the second with the full band. It becomes clear from this disc that Cobain didn't want to have the pop star mantle hanging over his head anymore, and it was eating away at his songwriting. A jam of 'Scentless Apprentice' paved the way for the classic piece of anger that followed, and almost makes the box set worth buying on its own. A bleak version of 'All Apologies', and a less-commercial version of 'Heart-Shaped Box' are also highlights.

Overall rating ★ ★ ★

Disc 4 (DVD) Tracklisting: 'Love Buzz' / 'Scoff' / 'About a Girl' / 'Big Long Now' / 'Immigrant Song' / 'Spank Thru' / 'Hairspray Queen' / 'School' / 'Mr. Moustache' (rehearsal from Krist Novoselic's mother's house, Aberdeen, 1988) / 'Big Cheese' (Los Angeles, 1989) / 'Sappy' (Long Beach, California, 1990) / 'In Bloom' (early music video) / 'School' (Seattle, 1990) / 'Love Buzz' (Seattle, 1990) / 'Pennyroyal Tea' / 'Smells Like Teen Spirit' / 'Territorial Pissings' (Seattle, 1991) / 'Jesus Doesn't Want Me for a Sunbeam' (Seattle, 1991) / 'Talk to Me' (Seattle, 1992) / 'Seasons in the Sun' (Rio de Janeiro, 1993)

The included DVD, spanning five years, starts with an early, fuzzy rehearsal from Novoselic's mother's house and ends with a performance of insipid '70s ballad 'Seasons in the Sun' from Rio de Janeiro. It is fascinating and insightful stuff.

Overall rating ★ ★ ★

Conclusion

With the Lights Out contains B-sides, rarities, and plentiful live footage over 3 CDs and a DVD. Containing more than 50 previously unreleased recordings spanning the length and breadth of their career, it is a valuable glimpse into the band's musical evolution. Much of the material here will only appeal to hardened fans, but it is undeniably a fascinating record of the group's creative processes. With the Lights Out is the highest-selling box set of all time, and it's not hard to see why.

Overall rating ★ ★ ★

CLASSIC ALBUMS - NIRVANA - NEVERMIND
(DVD, March 2005)

Sordid? Maybe. Absorbing and interesting? Sometimes. This documentary DVD from the Classic Albums series focuses on Nirvana's breakthrough album, Nevermind. Featuring interviews with Grohl, Novoselic, producer Butch Vig, and others on a variety of subjects, Nevermind is one of the better instalments in the series, which includes Pink Floyd's Dark Side of the Moon, and Fleetwood Mac's Rumours. Of special interest is the saga of how Grohl joined the band and the story behind the making of 'Drain You'. It's well worth a look.

Overall rating ★ ★ ★

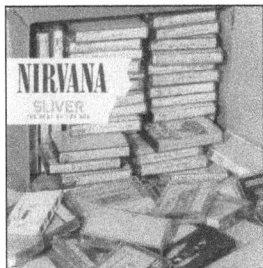

SLIVER: THE BEST OF THE BOX

(Compilation album, November 1, 2005)

Tracklisting: 'Spank Thru' (demo, 1985) / 'Heartbreaker' (live from Raymond, Washington, 1987) / 'Mrs. Butterworth' (demo, 1988) / 'Floyd the Barber' (live from Tacoma, Washington, 1988) / 'Clean Up Before She Comes' (demo, 1988) / 'About a Girl' (demo, 1988) / 'Blandest' (studio session from Seattle, 1988) / 'Ain't It a Shame' (studio session from Seattle, 1989 / 'Sappy' (studio session from Seattle, 1990) / 'Opinion' (KAOS radio show, 1990) / 'Lithium' (KAOS radio show, 1990) / 'Sliver' (demo, 1990) / 'Smells Like Teen Spirit' (demo, 1991) / 'Come as You Are' (demo, 1991) / 'Old Age' (Nevermind studio session, 1990) / 'Oh, the Guilt' (studio session from Seattle) / 'Rape Me' (acoustic demo, 1992) / 'Rape Me' (studio session from Seattle, 1992) / 'Heart-Shaped Box' (studio session from Rio de Janeiro, 1993) / 'Do Re Mi' (acoustic demo, 1994) / 'You Know You're Right' (acoustic demo, 1994) / 'All Apologies' (acoustic demo, undated)

Conclusion

The fourth, and I hope final, Nirvana album released since the band disbanded, and the most pointless one to boot. That's right, even more so than The Best Of … Containing 19 tracks culled from With the Lights Out, as well as three previously unreleased recordings, there's not much here to write home about. The booklet, however, manages to push the album up a star, containing, as it does, quotes provided by Novoselic that help us gain more insight into Nirvana's history. Even so, its certainly nothing special.

Overall rating ★ ★

ABOUT CODA BOOKS

Most Coda books are edited and endorsed by Emmy Award winning filmmaker and concert promoter Bob Carruthers. Over the last 20 years Bob has filmed and promoted tours, concerts and made documentaries all over Britain and Europe in venues ranging from Hammersmith Odeon to Murrayfield Stadium, with artists such as Bryan Adams, Spandau Ballet, Jethro Tull, Status Quo and Katherine Jenkins.

The 'Uncensored On the Record' series explores the careers of many of music's greatest legends, encompassing a wide range of genres including classic rock, pop, heavy metal, punk, country, classical and soul.

For more information visit **www.codabooks.com**.

BON JOVI
ON THE RECORD

THE EAGLES

ELVIS
UNCENSORED ON THE RECORD
BY ANTHONY MASSALY

GENESIS the GABRIEL ERA
UNCENSORED ON THE RECORD
BY BOB CARRUTHERS

GREEN DAY
UNCENSORED ON THE RECORD
Tom King

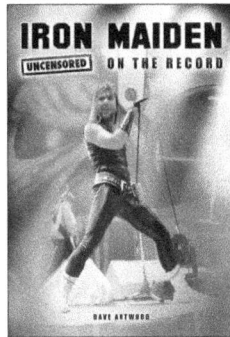

IRON MAIDEN
UNCENSORED ON THE RECORD
DAVE ARTWOOD

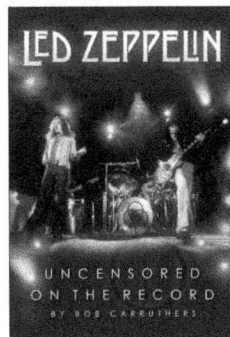

LED ZEPPELIN
UNCENSORED ON THE RECORD
BY BOB CARRUTHERS

METALLICA
UNCENSORED ON THE RECORD
BY TOM KING

NIRVANA
UNCENSORED ON THE RECORD
CAROL CLERK

PINK FLOYD
ON THE RECORD
BY BOB CARRUTHERS

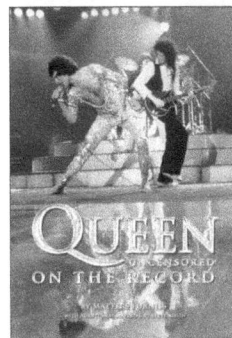

QUEEN
UNCENSORED ON THE RECORD

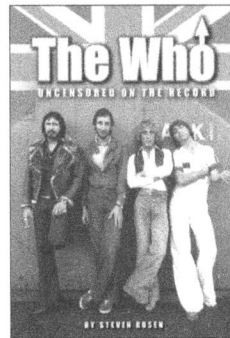

The Who
UNCENSORED ON THE RECORD
BY STEVEN ROSEN

www.ingramcontent.com/pod-product-compliance
Lightning Source LLC
Chambersburg PA
CBHW021144090426

42740CB00008B/940

* 9 7 8 1 7 8 1 5 8 2 4 7 3 *